Cannibal Island

HUMAN RIGHTS AND CRIMES AGAINST HUMANITY
Eric D. Weitz, Series Editor

Cannibal Island

Death in a Siberian Gulag

Nicolas Werth

Foreword by Jan T. Gross

Translated from the French by Steven Rendall

PRINCETON UNIVERSITY PRESS

PRINCETON AND OXFORD

Copyright © 2007 by Princeton University Press

Published by Princeton University Press, 41 William Street, Princeton,
New Jersey 08540

In the United Kingdom: Princeton University Press, 3 Market Place,
Woodstock, Oxfordshire OX20 1SY

First published in 2006 under the title *L'Île aux cannibales 1933, une
déportation-abandon en Sibérie* © by Perrin

Library of Congress Cataloging-in-Publication Data

Werth, Nicholas, 1950–
 [Île aux cannibales. English]
 Cannibal Island : death in a Siberian gulag / Nicholas Werth ; foreword
by Jan T. Gross ; tranlated from the French by Steven Rendall.
   p. cm.
 Includes bibliographical references.
 ISBN-13: 978-0-691-13083-5 (cl. : alk. paper)
 ISBN-10: 0-691-13083-3 (cl. : alk. paper)
   1. Ob River Region (Russia)—History—20th century. 2. Forced
migration—Russia (Federation)—Orb River Region—History—20th
century. 3. Political persecution—Soviet Union. 4. Concentration
camps—Soviet Union. 5. Political prisoners—Soviet Union. I. Title.

DK771.O2W4713 2007
365'.450947—dc22   2006051829

British Library Cataloging-in-Publication Data is available

This book has been composed in Méridien with Weiss display

Printed on acid-free paper. ∞

press.princeton.edu

Printed in the United States of America

10 9 8 7 6 5 4 3 2 1

It's not that death has no meaning here,
it's that life no longer has any value.
—Tzvetan Todorov, *Mémoire du mal:*
Tentation du bien

At this point, alas, we have to talk about
figures and statistics: it's painful to have
to calculate sordidly when a single death
suffices to constitute an absolute disaster.
—Annie Kriegel, *Les Communistes français:*
Essai d'éthnographie

Contents

Foreword
Jan T. Gross

Nicolas Werth, arguably the leading French historian of the Soviet era, is best known in the United States for his contribution to Stéphane Courtois' *The Black Book of Communism*. Werth has as solid a command of Soviet-era archival documentation as anyone. His writings are directly based on the original sources. Together with a team of Russian historians affiliated with Memorial (an organization documenting Stalinist terror in the Soviet Union), he prepared a seven-volume documentary history of the Gulag, which was published in 2004. He is a great writer in addition to being a top-notch historian. While laying out a synthetic, institutional panorama of a segment of Soviet bureaucracy, he can write at the same time a story full of suspense, in a crisp and lucid style. He certainly does both with shattering effect in his *Cannibal Island*.

This is a small and simple book that narrates, in essence, one episode from the universe of Stalinist repression: a deportation to Siberia in 1933 of several thousand city dwellers labeled as "socially harmful elements." But even for a reader like myself, who has leafed through thousands of pages of documents and writings on Stalinist terror, what Werth presents here comes as a numbing experience. This is a chapter from the saga of the "second," or "hidden," Gulag, that is, the forcible removal into the Soviet interior of millions of undesirables. The procedure started in earnest in the 1930s in the aftermath of collectivization and involved the transportation for settlement into one or another inhospitable region of entire categories of Soviet citizens classified as "special settlers." The so-called kulaks and their families led the way, but in time entire ethnic groups followed.

Rather than being put in labor camps, people subjected to this kind of repression were dumped in some far-away location (a "labor" or a "special" village), usually hundreds of kilometers from the nearest railway, and left to fend for themselves. The enthusiastic then-chief of the Soviet secret police, Genrikh Iagoda, foresaw the setting up of a thousand such villages, and calculated that "3,250 chekist village commanders" plus a set volume of construction materials would be needed to accommodate two million deportees. In short order they would help colonize virgin land, he argued, and would thus pay with all sorts of useful economic activity for their own upkeep and return the initial expenditure incurred to deport them. The vast majority of those who were eventually dispatched for such settlement arrived at the destination (many had already died on the way) utterly exhausted, and they found very little, or nothing at all, at the location where they were supposed to begin their new lives.

The island of Nazino "settlement" opened in May 1933 with nearly ten thousand people and twenty tons of flour, which was dumped in the open air on the riverbank rather than on the island, so that the famished deportees could not get to it all at once. In short order the flour, the only foodstuff available, went bad and what followed was human hell. By mid-June half of the deportees had disappeared—some died on the island, some drowned trying to flee across the River Ob. Those who made it to shore were for the most part killed by the population of a nearby village. They were famished and ready to eat anything, including human flesh, and people treated them like wild animals.

The story is well documented because it was investigated at the time by Soviet authorities. Werth's narrative reconstructs the process of negotiations by various segments of the Soviet bureaucracy that preceded the deportation as local officials tried to avoid responsibility for what they knew would end in disaster. This makes fascinating reading and opens up yet another point rarely mentioned in studies of the Stalinist era: namely, that as a result of collectivization and the ensuing famines and terror, there were hundreds of thousands of homeless people in the Soviet Union, vagabonds moving around the country and/or living marginal existences in larger towns. They lived outside of the law, such as it was, and were treated as human waste, which they in fact became as a result of state policies. Werth has given us in this slender volume a profound insight into a human-made human catastrophe of major proportions.

KARA SEA

Moscow

Ob

Yenisey

•Noril'sk

R U S S I A

Nazino
Island

Irtysh

Ob

Yenisey

Lena

•Tomsk

•Omsk

Novosibirsk•

•Krasnoyarsk

Lake Baikal

Astana•

Irkutsk•

Qaraghandy•

Ulaanbaatar•

KAZAKHSTAN

MONGOLIA

Lake Balkash

CHINA

Preface

V alery Fast is one of the founding members of the
Tomsk Memorial Association, an organization created during Gorbachev's perestroika in order to preserve
the memory of political repression in the USSR. On July
21, 1989, in the remote village of Nazino on the banks
of the Ob River in Western Siberia, he spoke with an
elderly peasant woman belonging to the Ostyak ethnic
group that had been living in this inhospitable region
since long before the Russians arrived. Here is what she
said:

> We were living in Ergankina. Every spring, we left for
> the island of Nazino to harvest the poplar bark that
> we sent downstream. It was our only source of in-
> come. The whole family went along, and we took
> enough food to spend the season there. That year,
> what did we see? People everywhere. They'd been
> brought to the island—it must have been in 1932, or
> rather 1933. In 1933, in the spring. I was thirteen. We
> came to the village of Nazino, which is on the river-
> bank across from the island. People said, "They've
> brought people to the island." How many? It turned
> out that there were about thirteen thousand of them.
> So many people! We didn't understand what was go-
> ing on. One thing was sure: the season was a bust for

us. They'd put them on the island, disembarked them in the middle of the night, all those people, I remember.

They were trying to escape. They asked us, "Where's the railway?" We'd never seen a railway. They asked, "Where's Moscow? Leningrad?" They were asking the wrong people: we'd never heard of those places. We're Ostyaks. People were running away, starving. They were given a handful of flour. They mixed it with water and drank it, and then they immediately got diarrhea. The things we saw! People were dying everywhere; they were killing each other. Alongside the river, near the village, there was a veritable mountain of flour. "You want some flour? Here you go!" They gave them just a handful.

On the island, there was a guard named Kostia Venikov, a young fellow. He was courting a pretty girl who had been sent there. He protected her. One day he had to be away for a while, and he told one of his comrades, "Take care of her," but with all the people there the comrade couldn't do much. . . . People caught the girl, tied her to a poplar tree, cut off her breasts, her muscles, everything they could eat, everything, everything. . . . They were hungry, they had to eat. When Kostia came back, she was still alive. He tried to save her, but she had lost too much blood— she died. The boy was out of luck. That was the kind of thing that happened. When you went along the island, you saw flesh wrapped in rags. Human flesh that had been cut and hung in the trees. I heard that when people on the island saw Iakim Ivanovich, the doctor, pass by, they said, "There's one that would be good to eat, fat as he is." He ran away. The militia took him away so they wouldn't eat him. Then he was arrested as an enemy of the people.

And yet, how much flour there was on the river-bank! They'd brought in a mountain of flour to feed people. But what they did with it, no one knows. One thing is certain: it rotted. Or maybe somebody stole it. I don't know whether it was stolen or not. What I do know is that people were starving to death.

They'd sent two guards to Ergankina along with their families in order to defend our village in case these . . . attacked us. As soon as the guards caught one, they put him on a boat and took him to the other side of the river, to Old Nazina. There they shot him and threw his body into the river, the current carried it away. There was the guard and Vassily Piatkin, a former convict who first settled in Nazina, and then came to live with us in Ergankina. They were the ones who took people over to the other bank and shot them. . . . On the way, they made them sing dirty songs. They threw them bread crumbs, and then made them sing again.

When the water went down, Irina went with the Tverertins to do the haying. Piotr Alexeievich Tveretin was the storekeeper in Ergankina, and Irina worked for him. When she came back from haying she told me, "What a stink, what a stink!" I saw that she was looking for something—she was constantly washing her hands, and then she went back to see the dead. I went into the fields, holding my Ostyak nose. She was right that it stank; the dead had decomposed—they'd been lying there for over a month. I understood that Tveretin and Irka were pulling gold teeth out of the corpses. "It's the boss who's making me do it," Irka said. There was a Torgsin[1] in Alexandrovskoie, but it no longer took payment in gold. Tveretin sold skins; he worked in the Sibpushina cooperative. He and his boss, Batalov, went to Tomsk to take gold to the Torgsin, and they didn't give Irina anything. In the Torgsin in Tomsk, they didn't care where the gold came from; they traded the gold for old clothes, macaroni, and all kinds of other food. Irina told me that. Today she lives in Tomsk. . . .

People fled the island on rafts, on tree trunks. One day, starving to death, hardly able to stand up, they tried to attack our cow. We went to stop them, and they took off; they started running and came to Ergankina. Starving. People thought they ought to give them a little bread. There were women among them, and that made us feel more confident. We said to the guards, "Let them alone, we'll give them something to eat." We took them home, gave them bread and milk. The guards had told us, "You can feed them, but don't let them go." We gave them bread, curds, milk, and then we took them back to the guardhouse. God knows that what they did with them afterward. Maybe they shot them, or they escaped, or they were taken back to the island.

My Lord, what cruelty! Of course, God knows what these people did. We didn't know them; they scared us. Still, when the guards were looking for them, we hid them for a couple of days. We brought them something to eat; we weren't animals. We gave them milk to drink, and fed them, and afterwards, they were shot.

At the end of the summer, before the cold weather came, they put the people who were still alive on a big barge. They loaded as many as they could and then started down the Nazina River. Almost all of them died. The survivors, they probably took them somewhere. They left on a barge on the Nazina. They dug *zemlianki*.[2] Anyone can tell you what these *zemlianki* looked like. Later on, they built real houses out of wood and even a meeting house and a bridge over the river. Old Kondratii told me that. Then they started letting people go. God knows where they went. . . . I don't know who's still alive.

With this testimony—complemented and confirmed by a dozen others collected on Nazino and in neighboring villages[3]—rises to the surface a crucial and particularly dramatic episode that has been ignored for almost six decades: the deportation in 1933 of thousands of "déclassé and socially harmful elements" from Moscow and Leningrad who were left to their fates on a little island not far from the confluence of the Ob and the Nazina Rivers, some 800 kilometers north of the Siberian city of Tomsk. Since the early 1990s, the opening-up of the regional archives in Novosibirsk and Tomsk, along with the publication of certain documents concerning the tragedy of Nazino, has allowed us to see more clearly what happened on "Dead Island" (*Ostrov-Smert*), which the locals also called "Cannibal Island" (*Ostrov lioudoedov*). In 2002, a crucial step was taken with the publication of the documents produced by the commission of inquiry set up in September 1933 by the Regional Committee of the Communist Party of Western Siberia.[4] The commission's goal was to "check the veracity of the information that Comrade Velichko, the Party's journalist-propagandist in the Narym region, sent to Comrade Stalin regarding the situation that occurred on the island of Nazino, on the Ob." Had this base-level Communist official not decided to undertake his own investigation into the circumstances under which thousands of deportees had died, and then dared to write to Stalin himself, no committee would have brought these events to light.

Thanks to the documents produced by the commission of inquiry, it is now possible to reconstitute in detail the mechanisms leading to this "deportation-abandonment" and to understand better how the system of "special settlements" set up in haste in early 1930 functioned at the local level. How was this event situated in the policy of massive deportations Stalin's regime had been pursuing for more than three years in an effort to "liquidate the kulaks as a class"? Why and how had "déclassé and socially harmful elements" rounded up in Moscow and Leningrad been deported to this isolated, virtually inaccessible region more than 800 kilometers from the nearest city and or railway line? Who were these "elements"? Was the Nazino tragedy "programmed," or was it instead the result of extraordinary mismanagement, a total lack of coordination between the different links in the repressive system of the "Second Gulag," the one that involved "special settlers and labor colonists"? Was it a unique, extreme case of "deportation-abandonment"?

For Ivan Ivanovich Dolguikh, the head of the Siblag[5] Department of Special Settlements, in this episode there was nothing "extreme" but the behavior of the "déclassés" themselves, who were truly the "dregs of humanity indulging in cannibalism." "In 1930, in the middle of November, we'd settled five thousand kulaks without shelter in the taiga, in a snow-covered, empty region," he told the commission, "and there were no political consequences [*sic*] because this contingent immediately began constructing shelters and managed to survive perfectly well."[6] This is a remarkable acknowledgment that says a great deal about the way the highest officials responsible for the deportation of "kulaks" conceived the management of "contingents." The latter were to owe their survival to their own initiative and their ability to surmount the worst ordeals.

In reality, as the following microhistorical effort to reconstitute this event will try to show, the uniqueness of what happened on the island of Nazino had to do with a very particular conjunction of circumstances: an unusual group of "special settlers" deported at the beginning of a vast campaign of social engineering based on a utopian plan to colonize the vast virgin areas of Siberia and Kazakhstan. This plan was so "grandiose" (the adjective used by its author, Genrikh Iagoda, the head of the OGPU,[7] to describe it) that it caught officials unprepared at all levels of the Special Settlements Department and clearly revealed all the dysfunctions of the system that had been laboriously set up over the preceding years to "manage dekulakization." In the end, the "grandiose plan" elaborated in early 1933 was implemented only to a very limited extent. After a few months, the repressive machinery having proven incapable of "digesting" the contingents, and the coordination between the Center and the periphery falling victim to an increasing number of failures, the large-scale deportations came to an end, at least for a few years. It is a tragic irony of history that the Nazino episode took place only a few days after Stalin had largely shelved the "grandiose plan" for deportation that the head of the political police had drawn up for him a few months earlier!

In its extreme brutality (two-thirds of the deportees died of hunger, exhaustion, and disease in the weeks following their abandonment), a brutality that was to lead to transgressions such as cannibalism and necrophagy, the Nazino episode was extraordinary and deeply revelatory of the climate of violence and regression that in the early 1930s swept over certain Soviet areas that had been deeply disturbed by massive deportations and exoduses, suffered endemic food shortages and even famines, and were prey to roving bands of outlaws in the countryside and renewed outbreaks of criminality in the cities. Among these areas figured especially Western Siberia, a sort of Soviet "Far East," a place of deportation and house arrest for those excluded from the socialist society that was being built; it was both a frontier region and a garbage can.

Glossary

GULAG: The main administrative agency for the camps, created in 1930. The Gulag managed both the labor camps and the "special villages."

KOMANDATURA: An administrative agency under the Gulag's Department of Special Settlements responsible for managing persons deported and put under house arrest in their place of exile (the special villages). In the late 1930s, there were over 1,800 komandaturas responsible for supervising more than a million special settlers.

OGPU: The overall state political administration. Since 1922, this term had in fact designated the Soviet regime's political police. The OGPU included the GPUs (state political administrations) of each federated socialist republic constituting the USSR. From 1917 to 1922, the new regime's political police was known as Vecheka (abbreviated Cheka), the All-Russian Extraordinary Commission for Combating Counterrevolution, Speculation, and Sabotage. In 1934, the OGPU was absorbed into the NKVD (People's Commissariat of Internal Affairs).

Cannibal Island

CHAPTER 1

A *"grandiose plan"*

In early February 1933, Genrikh Iagoda, the head of the OGPU, and Matvei Berman, the head of the Gulag,[1] presented Stalin with a vast plan for deporting millions of "anti-Soviet elements in the cities and the countryside" to Western Siberia and Kazakhstan. They explained that the experience acquired over the preceding three years, during which more than two million "kulaks"[2] had been deported, made it possible to move on to a new, much more extensive effort to deport "all the elements polluting the socialist society currently being constructed." In 1933–34, a million "elements" were to be settled in Western Siberia, and as many in Kazakhstan.

Six categories were targeted:

1. kulaks who had not yet been "dekulakized" in the course of the preceding years;[3]
2. peasants (including those who had joined kolkhozes) who were "sabotaging the state's procurement plans and other politico-economic campaigns undertaken by the state";
3. "kulaks who are hiding in firms and workplaces or escaping from the countryside";

4. "individuals expelled in the context of cleaning up the USSR's western frontiers";
5. "urban elements refusing to leave cities in the context of "passportization";[4]
6. individuals whom the courts and the OGPU's special jurisdictions had sentenced to terms of less than five years, with the exception of "elements particularly dangerous from a social point of view."

All these "elements" deported as "labor colonists" (a new label) would have the same status as the "kulaks" deported in 1930–31 (labeled "special settlers"): they would be deprived of their civil rights, put under house arrest in a "labor village," and put to special—and specially harsh—use within state economic structures responsible for exploiting the timber, mining, and agricultural resources of the Soviet "Far East."

According to Genrikh Iagoda's plan, 75 percent of the labor colonists—that is, about one and a half million people—were to work on farms and in the forests. Within two years, .hey were supposed to have "freed the state from any expense for their support and begun producing merchandise that would allow the state to recover the expenses incurred in the operations of deportation and settlement of the contingents." The rest— some five hundred thousand people—were to work in the sectors of fishing, crafts, and mining, "while at the same time conducting a small side operation in order to feed themselves."

To ensure the success of this deportation-colonization,

which was intended to bring into production at least a million hectares of virgin land, one thousand labor villages (at the rate of one village for every two thousand "elements" or about five hundred families) would be built. Each village would consist of a hundred living units of 650 square feet each, sheltering twenty people (each deportee thus being allotted 27 square feet of living space). During the first year, baths, an infirmary, a hygienic station for removing "lice and other parasites," stables, and a garage for machinery were to be constructed; during the second year, a school, a cafeteria, a reading room, a store, and so on. For the construction of these labor villages, the managers of the OGPU and the Gulag estimated that they would need 3,385,000 cubic meters of wood, 10,288 metric tons of iron and sheet metal, 6,929 metric tons of nails, 2,591 square meters of glass, and other materials.

These labor villages (which differed only in name from the special villages to which dekulakized persons had been sent over the preceding three years) were to be administered by a "chekist-commander" with very broad powers. Some 3,250 of these chekist-commanders and "assistants" were to be recruited, along with 5,700 militiamen, 1,000 technicians, 500 agronomists, and 470 physicians and health officers. The whole administrative, police, and economic management of the labor villages would be the exclusive responsibility of a main managerial office specially created to run the labor villages.

"The most delicate problem," the head of the OGPU and the head of the Gulag acknowledged, "is the transportation of the human contingents and equipment—construction materials, livestock and tools, the food supplies authorized to ensure the contingents' survival—from the point were the rail lines or waterways end to the places assigned for the contingents' residence and economic implementation. Since these places are all situated in practically uninhabited regions, we cannot count on local means of transportation. Preliminary estimates drawn up by our offices set the needs, so far as transportation goes, at 2,416 trucks, on the basis of a daily transportation of three metric tons of freight over a distance of 250 kilometers roundtrip per day; 90,000 horses, considering that one horse should be able to plow ten hectares and that in addition to this work, the horses will be used to transport wood; 1,200 tractors to be used both for agricultural work and for transporting freight and contingents."

The plan presented by Iagoda and Berman ended with a long list of expenses and the contributions, in cash and in kind, to be asked from a half-dozen ministries and other state committees. The total expense—described as "absolutely minimal, based on the experience acquired during the operations of deportation and accommodation of special settlers in 1930–31, but in absolute numbers, truly grandiose, since it covers no less than the settlement of two million almost completely deprived individuals in virgin territories hundreds of kilometers away from any railway"—was estimated at 1,394 million rubles.

The highest officials in the repressive system were probably aware of the enormity of the sum requested and the "grandiose scope" of the project envisioned. This is shown by a few concluding lines typed in capital letters:

THE SUM OF THESE MONETARY EXPENSES, CON-
STRUCTION MATERIALS, LIVESTOCK, MEANS OF
TRANSPORTATION, AND FOOD SUPPLIES FOR PEO-
PLE AND ANIMALS COMMITTED TO THE PROJECT
IS SO GRANDIOSE THAT A SPECIAL COMMITTEE
MUST BE SET UP TO REFINE THE NEEDS AND PLANS
FOR THE DEPORTATION AND SETTLEMENT OF THE
CONTINGENTS.[5]

To understand the meaning, place, and scope of this
"grandiose plan," we must briefly recall the context at
the beginning of 1933. The situation had been very tense
since the summer of 1932. In order to guarantee large-
scale exports of grains and other agricultural products
that would make it possible to import the equipment required for accelerated industrialization in the country,
the Party leadership once again raised the targets for
obligatory deliveries imposed on the kolkhozes as well
as on "individual" peasants—despite the fact that a poor
harvest was predicted and that many reports from
Ukraine, the North Caucasus, the Volga region, Western
Siberia, and Kazakhstan mention "isolated areas where
there are problems with food supply"—a formula that
masks a far more dramatic reality: genuine shortages
pointing toward a coming famine. The 1932 procurement campaign, begun in July, was stalled; in mid-October, only 15–20 percent of the planned obligatory deliveries from the main grain-producing regions of the
country had come in. The peasants, often with the com-
plicity of the kolkhoz's management, used all kinds of
stratagems to avoid delivering part of the harvest to the
state: "thefts of the collective harvest" multiplied (de-

spite the promulgation in August 1932 of a draconian law punishing theft of "social property" by ten years of forced labor in camps—or the death penalty. Wheat was buried in pits, hidden in "black granaries,"[6] ground in homemade "hand mills," and stolen during transportation or weighing. What was particularly disturbing for the Stalinist ruling elite was the solidarity many kolkhoz managers showed with the people they were supposed to be managing, and even overt opposition to the state's procurement plans on the part of a certain number of local Party and Soviet officials, especially in the great agricultural regions that were most heavily levied, such as Ukraine, the Kuban, and the Volga area. In order to put an end to this resistance, in 1932 the highest level of the party leadership, the Politburo, sent two "extraordinary committees" to Ukraine and the North Caucasus. One of these committees was headed by Vyacheslav Molotov, the other by Lazar Kaganovich. Thousands of OGPU agents and Party "plenipotentiaries" were mobilized and dispatched from urban to rural areas in order to compensate for the failures of the local Communist authorities. During the summer of 1932, the country was overtaken by a climate of extreme violence that recalled the worst aspects of the "dekulakization" campaign of early 1930: hundreds of thousands of "saboteurs of the procurement plan" were arrested. The repression was so excessive that it sometimes lost all meaning. One of many similar reports on the situation, addressed by an official from the grain-producing region of the Lower Volga to his superiors in early 1933, bears eloquent testimony to this fact:

Arrests and searches are carried out by anyone at all: members of the rural soviet, emissaries of all kinds, members of the shock brigades, any komsomol who isn't too lazy. . . . According to calculations made by the former assistant prosecutor in the district, Comrade Vassiliev, over the past year, 15 percent of the adult population has been the victim of one kind of repression or another. If to that we add that in the course of the past month about eight hundred farmers have been expelled from the kolkhozes, you'll have some idea of the scope of the repression in this district. If we exclude cases in which the repression is justified, it has to be said that the efficacy of the repressive measures is constantly diminishing, since when they go beyond a certain threshold, it becomes difficult to carry them out. . . . Yesterday I met a large number of kolkhozians who had been expelled from the kolkhoz at the beginning of February, and then taken back at the end of the month. Expelling people from the kolkhoz no longer has any effect. It's almost the same with criminal prosecutions. In February, more than four thousand persons were convicted in the district. All the prisons are jammed full. The Balachevo Prison is holding five times as many people as it was planned for, and at Elan, the district prison is currently holding 610 people. Over the past month, the Balachevo Prison "returned" to Elan seventy-eight convicts, forty-eight of whom were under the age of ten; twenty-one were immediately released. What effect on the population can be produced by our extremely repressive laws and judges, when we know that at the prosecution's suggestion, 120 persons sentenced to two years' and more imprisonment for sabotaging the procurement campaign have had to be set free because of the overcrowding of the prisons and have gone home? . . . To close my remarks on this method, the only one in use here—the method of force—a few words about the individual peasants[7] with regard to whom everything is done to discourage them from sowing and producing. . . .

"The individual peasant—he's an enemy of Soviet power, and so he can be treated however one wants"—that's the opinion of the local officials regarding this question. The following example shows how terrorized the individual peasants are: in Mortsy, an individual peasant who had nonetheless met his planned target 100 percent came to see Comrade Fomichev, the president of the district's executive committee and asked to be deported, for, in any event, he explained, "you can't live under these conditions any longer." Similarly exemplary is the petition, signed by sixteen individual peasants of the rural soviet of Alexandrov, in which these peasants ask to be deported outside their region! Mass labor is nonexistent. The only form of mass labor is the "assault": seeds, funds, livestock raising are "taken by assault," people "launch an assault" on work. Nothing is now done without an "assault." You can no longer count all the "shock brigades." The latter usually consist of a district official, a member of the rural soviet, a team leader, and two or three kolkhozians. They "attack" at night, from nine or ten in the evening until dawn. The "attack" takes place as follows: the "shock brigade," using a hut as its headquarters, "convokes" one after another all the people who have not fulfilled one or another obligation or plan and "convinces" them, by various means, to honor their obligations. In this way, each person on the list is "attacked," and this goes on all night. The kolkhozians have become so accustomed to this practice that they no longer do anything without a "shock brigade."[8]

Thanks to "assaults," the procurement plan was completely fulfilled at the beginning of 1933, but at what cost! In the producing regions most heavily levied, the kolkhozes were able to meet the targets only by giving up their "seed stocks," their last reserves that allowed them to provide for the next harvest and to give emergency aid to starving kolkhozians. Starting in 1933, shortages and then famine swept over a large part of Ukraine, the North Caucasus, and the Volga region.

It was in this context that an important plenary meeting of the Central Committee, a major annual session bringing together the Party's leading officials, took place in Moscow, January 7–12, 1933. On the agenda were especially the balance sheet for the first five-year plan and the future outlook. Despite a particularly alarming situation in the agricultural sector and an "overheating" of industrial investment, all the political officials, including the leaders of the Ukrainian Communist Party, some of whom had tried to resist Moscow's pressure, celebrated the "triumph of socialism" and the "spectacular success of the first five-year plan, carried out in four years and three months." In his speech, Stalin developed a new "theory," which can be summed up in a simple idea: with the triumph of socialism and the liquidation of the exploiting classes, oppositions did not disappear; they took different forms. Defeated, the enemies of socialism no longer acted overtly. Masked, veritable mutants, they were carrying on a particularly vicious "war of sabotage" that could take forms that were unexpected and difficult to recognize. Some would carry out their sabotage within the kolkhoz itself; others would leave the kolkhozes in large numbers and spread false rumors to discredit collectivized farming, while still others would infiltrate factories or major construction sites in order to carry out acts of sabotage. Weakened, the "debris of the exploiting classes" would seek to ally themselves with "déclassé elements," criminals, and other marginal groups. Henceforth, criminality and social deviance would constitute the chief threat to the construction of socialism.[9]

At the very time that this plenary session was taking place, the exodus of peasants from areas affected by the famine was growing. The OGPU's regional directors were certain that all these departures were "carefully organized by counterrevolutionary organizations." "In one week, our services have arrested five hundred hardened agitators who were urging the peasants to leave," wrote Vsevolod Balitski, the head of Ukraine's political police, to Genrikh Iagoda.[10] On January 22, Stalin composed, in the name of the Party's Central Committee and the government, a secret directive ordering that an end be put to the massive exodus of peasants fleeing Ukraine and the North Caucasus "on the pretext of going to look for bread." "The Central Committee and the Council of the People's Commissars," Stalin wrote, "has proof that this exodus from Ukraine was organized by enemies of Soviet power, by socialist revolutionaries and Polish agents, for propaganda purposes, in order to discredit, through the intermediary of peasants fleeing toward regions of the USSR north of Ukraine, the kolkhozian system in particular and the Soviet system in general."[11] The same day, Iagoda sent the OGPU's regional directors a circular ordering that special patrols be set up, especially in railway stations and on highways, to intercept all "runaways" coming from Ukraine and the North Caucasus. After "filtering" the intercepted individuals, the "kulak and counterrevolutionary elements," individuals "propagating counterrevolutionary rumors regarding alleged food shortages," and all those who refused to return home should be arrested and deported to labor villages (or, for the "most hardened among them," dispatched to a camp). The other runaways would be "sent home"—a measure that condemned them to certain death in villages that were suffering from famine and had been left entirely to their fate, without the slightest aid in securing food.[12]

As early as the following day, January 23, the operation seeking to prevent starving people from fleeing (and from spreading news about a famine denied by the authorities) was completed by directives suspending the sale of train tickets to peasants.[13] In the course of the last week of January, some twenty-five thousand refugees were arrested. A report drawn up two months after the operation began mentioned more than two hundred twenty-five thousand persons apprehended. Although the great majority of the peasants intercepted were "sent home," tens of thousands of them were interned in improvised "filtering" centers while waiting to be deported as labor colonists.[14] Also waiting to be deported were tens of thousands of other peasants (and also minor rural officials) arrested since the end of 1932 for "sabotage of the procurement campaign."[15]

Simultaneously, vast police operations were launched in January–February 1933 in the western border regions from western Ukraine to Belorussia, and also in Karelia, on the border between Finland and the USSR. Since the great peasant insurrections that had taken place in the spring of 1930, the frontier districts of western Ukraine, which bordered on Poland, were considered to be "lairs of Petlyurians"[16] in the pay of the Polish government. Stalin's obsession with the "Polish enemy" was permanent, as is shown, for example, by his directive of January 22, 1933 cited above. In a few weeks, the OGPU arrested, in the borderlands of western Ukraine, some 9,500 persons, most of them peasants described as "kulaks" and accused of belonging to "Petlyurian-Polish insurrectional organizations."[17] Similar operations led to the arrest of 3,500 persons in the border districts of Belorussia. Finally, more than 2,000 persons, again most of them peasants, were arrested in Karelia on the pretext that they belonged to "insurrectional cells set up by the Finnish general staff."[18] For the head of the OGPU, the operations launched in early 1933 obviously constituted only the first stage of a broad "cleansing" (*ocistka*) of the western borderlands, which explains the inclusion of the contingent of "individuals expelled in the framework of cleansing the USSR's western frontiers" as one of the six categories targeted by the major deportation plan of February 1933.

The conjunction of all these repressive campaigns led to massive "congestion" in the prisons, especially in areas where the operations of agricultural collection had been the harshest—Ukraine, the North Caucasus, along the Volga, and in the Black Earth. Since the establishment of labor camps and special villages for "relocated peasants,"[19] the prisons, whose maximal capacity was on the order of 180,000 inmates, commonly took in prisoners sentenced to short terms (less than three years) and arrested individuals who were awaiting judgment. Starting in the summer of 1932, under the impact of the massive arrests connected with the procurement campaign, which was particularly tense, the number of people incarcerated increased exponentially, reaching the enormous figure of 800,000 in the spring of 1933. In February 1933, Nikolay Krylenko, the people's commissar in the Justice Department, proposed to "decongest" the prisons and to settle several hundred thousand inmates in labor villages. At the beginning of March 1933, the Politburo approved Krylenko's proposal.[20] Priority was to be given to the prisons in Ukraine, the North Caucasus, the central area of the Black Earth, and the lower Volga, all regions where the concentration of inmates was such that it could at any time lead to serious disturbances of public order, since the overcrowded prisons were scarcely guarded and the prisoners received ridiculously scant rations at the very moment when famine was spreading rapidly in the countryside and in the cities. Over the following two months, 57,000 inmates sen-

tenced to terms of more than three years were to be
transferred to labor camps; 83,000 inmates serving lesser
terms were to be deported to labor villages, with the
same status as the kulaks deported during the preceding
years.[21]

In reality, these transfers represented only the first stage
of a larger process that was to expand considerably in
the course of 1933. Naturally, this policy of "decongest-
ing" the prisons was also applied to places of detention in
large cities affected by the "passportization" of the urban
population begun in January 1933. In connection with
this policy, hundreds of thousands of "undesirable elements" were driven out of the cities, and many of them
were deported to labor villages.

The "passportization" of the urban population, a bureaucratic and police operation of unexampled breadth (in a
little more than a year, no less than twenty-seven million
city dwellers received a passport, which was to replace all
other attestations of identity previously delivered by the
most diverse authorities), had several objectives.

The first objective was to control migratory movements and to limit the immense rural exodus triggered
by the forced collectivization of the countryside. The
massive influx into the cities of millions of peasants[22]
fleeing the "second serfdom" threatened the whole system of rationing for the urban population that had been
laboriously set up since 1929. At the beginning of 1930
some twenty-six million city dwellers had a claim on
these rations; by the end of 1930 the number of claim-
ants rose to almost forty million.

The second objective was to better identify individuals, "to establish with exactitude their social position" in a society where up to that point there had been no standardized document of identity, the use of an interior passport having been rejected in 1917 as one of the most odious legacies of the Czarist regime. In order to prove their identities, Soviet citizens could present a birth certificate; a certificate provided by the soviet of their place of residence; a professional, trade union, or Party card; a certificate of residence provided by the cooperative of their apartment building; or any other official document delivered by a government office.[23]

The third objective was to "cleanse Moscow, Leningrad, and the other great urban centers of the USSR of superfluous elements not connected with production or administrative work, as well as kulaks, criminals, and other antisocial and socially dangerous elements."[24] This measure, significantly, was also to affect the main resorts frequented by the *nomenklatura*, Sochi and Tuapse on the Black Sea and the spas of the Caucasus (Mineralnye Vody, Kislovodsk).[25]

"The passport," Iagoda emphasized, "is the first and chief line of social defense against criminals and socially harmful elements."[26] The idea of "purifying" cities—and especially Moscow and Leningrad, the strategic loci of power—by cleansing them of their "antisocial elements," also designated by the terms "parasites," "déclassés," "socially dangerous," and "socially harmful," recurrently appears in Bolshevist discourse and practice, even in the years of the New Economic Policy (NEP), which were marked by a relative relaxation of political and social tensions.

What did the notion of "social dangerousness" mean in Bolshevist political culture? The term began to appear explicitly in 1924, when a secret resolution passed on March 24 of that year by the Soviet state's highest authority, the Central Executive Committee of the USSR, authorized a special jurisdiction, the OGPU's Special Conference, to ban, exile, expel outside the country, or put in a concentration camp for a maximum term of three years any "socially dangerous" individual. Such persons were defined as those who had been found guilty or suspected of "crimes of state" ("counterrevolutionary activities," larceny, counterfeiting); certain individuals "without fixed occupation and not engaged in productive work," such as "professional gamblers," "wheeler-dealers," pimps, drug dealers, "hardened speculators"; and all individuals who were "socially dangerous because of their past activities, that is, who had at least twice been found guilty of crimes or who had been arrested at least four times because of their suspected involvement in crimes against goods or persons."[27] This text is remarkable in several respects, not only because of its very elastic definition of "social dangerousness," which went beyond the well-known amalgamation—carried out at the beginnings of the regime—of "political offenders" and "nonpolitical offenders," but also because of its deterministic vision of "social dangerousness" as situated in the past and present history of "hardened" recidivists "connected with the crime world," a vision very different from the utopian approach fashionable in certain judicial and pedagogical circles that preached the "redemption of the criminal through labor."

Until the end of the 1920s, the impact of this law remained relatively limited, at least on the scale of the repression that would be carried out during the following decade. As early as the summer of 1924, however, the OGPU's new prerogatives were applied to some forty-five hundred "socially dangerous elements" expelled from Moscow and Leningrad upon completion of a vast police roundup.

Two years later, in May 1926, Feliks Dzerjinski sent his assistant, Genrikh Iagoda, an ambitious program for cleaning up the capital:

> It is necessary to cleanse Moscow of its parasitical elements. . . . I've asked Pauker[28] to collect all the available documentation concerning the creation of files on Moscow residents with regard to this problem. For the moment, I haven't received anything from him. Don't you think that within the OGPU a special colonization department should be created, financed by a special fund drawn from confiscations? The parasitical and socially dangerous elements in our cities (including their families) have to be used to populate the country's inhospitable areas, in accord with a plan prepared beforehand by the government. We must at all costs cleanse our cities of the hundreds of thousands of parasites that are flourishing there and eating us alive. . . . The OGPU must grapple with this problem, with the greatest energy."[29]

Analogous plans for "cleansing" cities of their "socially dangerous elements" or "parasites" (beggars, vagabonds, homeless children, minor delinquents, "speculators," traffickers, and also recidivist criminals) were drawn up in various provincial cities (in Leningrad in 1926; in Kharkov and Odessa in 1927; in the main Siberian cities, Novosibirsk, Tomsk, and Omsk, in 1928–29).[30]

Nonetheless, until the end of the 1920s the number of "socially dangerous elements" banished by decree of an OGPU special jurisdiction remained relatively modest on a national scale: about eleven thousand in 1927, twenty-eight thousand in 1929. Of this number, the "political offenders" represented a small minority—between 20 and 25 percent of the exiles, most of the latter being "nonpolitical offenders."[31]

In reality, the banishment and exile of "socially dangerous elements" raised more problems than it solved. "Under the current circumstances," in 1927 an official in the Interior Ministry wrote,

> the exile of socially dangerous elements, far from attaining its goal, is proving harmful to public order: its only result is to shift these elements from one province to another. . . . In general, socially dangerous elements are unable to find work in their place of exile, and so they immediately return to their criminal or suspect activities, rejoining the army of local criminals, whose ranks they further strengthen, transforming whole districts into zones in which Soviet power becomes incapable of maintaining public order.[32]

However, in late 1932, confronted by the growing chaos resulting from the influx of millions of peasants fleeing collectivization and besieging the large cities, the authorities decided finally to implement, within the framework of the policy of the passportization of the urban population, the ambitious program of "cleansing Moscow" Feliks Dzerjinski had recommended in 1926. But this program of identifying individuals was now to be far broader and more systematic, including expulsion of undesirable elements and in some cases their deportation to special villages.

On December 28, 1932, *Pravda* published the decrees, which the Politburo had ratified on the preceding day, instituting an internal passport, henceforth obligatory for Soviet citizens over the age of sixteen who were permanent residents of the cities or the worker's housing complexes, or were active in transportation or certain major construction projects considered to be strategic. The passport holder had to present his document at the local police station in his place of residence in order for it to be duly registered. Only registration (*propiska*) validated the passport, thus setting up a double monitoring of the passport holder's identity and legal place of residence. The operations of passportization were to be carried out first in the cities of Moscow, Leningrad, Kharkov, Kiev, Odessa, Minsk, Rostov-on-the-Don, Vladikavkaz, Magnitogorsk, and Vladivostok.[33] In these cities, designated as subject to a "special regime," the operation was to proceed by stages, beginning with people employed in firms and ending with the "nonorganized population," that is, those who had no strong connection, or no connection at all, with a workplace, a population that was a priori suspicious in the eyes of the authorities.

A secret directive defined seven vaguely delimited categories of individuals to whom passports should be refused in these "special regime" cities:

1. Individuals not working in production or an institution and not engaged in some form of socially useful labor (with the exception of retirees and the handicapped).

2. Kulaks and dekulakized individuals who had fled the place to which they had been deported, including those who were working in a firm or Soviet institution.
3. Individuals who had come from the countryside or another city after January 1, 1931 without a formal invitation issued by a firm or Soviet institution, and currently without employment or who are employed but are clearly good-for-nothings, or who had been fired in the past because they had disturbed production.
4. Individuals who have been stripped of their civil rights (*lichentsy*).[34]
5. Individuals who have been sentenced to deprivation of their freedom or to exile, as well as all antisocial elements maintaining relationships with criminals.
6. Refugees of foreign origin, with the exception of political refugees.
7. Family members of individuals designated above and living in the same household.[35]

Persons to whom a passport had been denied were required to leave the city and its environs within ten days (in the case of Moscow and Leningrad, the operations of passportization included a suburban and rural zone 100 kilometers in diameter). These persons were authorized to settle in any other locality not subject to the "special regime." To implement the population's passportization, the government created a new general department of the militia, directly under the OGPU. More than twelve thousand additional police officers were hired. "Passport offices" were set up in each firm, government agency, and local police station.

As might be imagined, the issuance of passports gave rise to countless abuses and irregularities, given the vagueness of the definition of the categories of people considered undesirable.[36] During the first two months of the passportization campaign (March–April 1933), seventy thousand persons who had applied for a passport were refused and had to leave Moscow; in Leningrad, more than seventy-three thousand refusals were registered.[37] As one OGPU official—G. Prokofiev, the head of the militia—noted, this left unresolved the problem of

the enormous number of déclassé and socially dangerous elements living illegally in Moscow and Leningrad and polluting these cities. When the passportization operation was announced, these individuals, knowing perfectly well that they would not be issued a passport, did not spontaneously present themselves in the passport offices and instead hid in attics, sheds, cellars, gardens, etc. . . . In order to capture and immediately and permanently expel all these individuals, the passport office's special militias, operating under the aegis of the inspector of the relevant sector, check the lists kept by concierges and building superintendents, make the rounds of the barracks for seasonal workers, places where unsavory elements hang out, illegal overnight shelters, attics and cellars, and conduct roundups in train stations, markets, bazaars, and other populous places in order to extirpate the déclassé elements, beggars, and thieves.[38]

Thanks to these operational steps, Prokofiev concludes, 85,937 individuals living in Moscow without a passport, along with 4,776 individuals living in Leningrad without a passport, had been arrested and sent to a camp or deported to a special labor village between March and July 1933.[39]

Individuals arrested without a passport were subject to a particularly summary administrative procedure. Within forty-eight hours, the sector inspector sent a list of the persons arrested to a special police committee (called *passportnaia troika*) whose sole task was to "deal in an extrajudicial manner with matters connected with passportization." These committees were authorized to sentence offenders, without having to summon those who had violated passport laws, to several kinds of penalties: immediate expulsion, with a prohibition on residing in thirty cities; deportation to a special village, where they would be under house arrest; or being sent to a labor camp for a maximum term of three years. These penalties were effective immediately and could not be appealed.

In reality, many of the people arrested during the police roundups did not even go through these summary procedures, and were directly deported after a short stay in a transit prison. This was the case for many individuals deported from Leningrad and Moscow, in the framework of the "cleansing" of the USSR's two largest cities on the occasion of Labor Day, May 1, 1933. They were sent to Tomsk, and then, after a short stay in the largest transit camp for special settlers en route to Siberia, to the island of Nazino.

CHAPTER 2

Western Siberia, a Land of Deportation

On February 7, 1933, the OGPU's plenipotentiary representative in Western Siberia, Alexiev, the regional head of the political police, received a telegram signed by Genrikh Iagoda informing him of the imminent deportation, "between winter and summer of this year," of a new contingent of one million people. This contingent was to be settled "as far as possible from any railway," that is, in the northern districts, and especially in the immense forests and marshes of the Narym region, which covered almost 350,000 square kilometers. It was specified that the deportees were to work in agriculture, fishing, and forestry, and that within two years the state was to be "completely freed of any need to provide supplies for this contingent." As for the concrete details of this vast operation, the regional OGPU authorities were expected, *within two days*, to provide Moscow with the following information:

1. The places suitable for settling the deportees, along with the number of families that could be settled in each district;
2. the lands available, and their quality;

3. potentialities for development—agriculture, fishing, craftwork;
4. data regarding the number of sovkhozes (soviet farms) considered by the local authorities to be unpromising, and that could be put back into production by contingents of deportees;
5. needs—in cash, construction materials, and so forth—that had to be met for the settlement of the deportees. A budget for supply, transportation, farm tools, tractors, seed, and productive livestock to get farming started;
6. how to organize a smooth transfer of individuals and merchandise;
7. concrete proposals for using specific existing villages to house a first wave of 100,000 deportees, to be carried out during the winter;
8. manpower needs to manage the contingent (guards, police officers, etc.);
9. proposals for organizing transfers (by river or road) after the rail convoys had been unloaded;
10. availability of and needs for health personnel and medicines;
11. needs for local means of transportation.[1]

Obviously, all these questions indicated that the "grandiose plan" for deportation had been improvised *na khodu* (on the spur of the moment)—a way of proceeding that was not unusual in economic "planning" during these years. Two days later, Iagoda's telegram was discussed at the highest regional political level, in the Office of the Party Committee of Western Siberia led by Robert Eikhe, and in the presence of the OGPU's plenipotentiary representative and two of the highest officers of the Siblag, the Siberian branch of the Gulag responsible for managing labor camps and special villages. The Committee categorically rejected the deportation plan, "deeming it absolutely impossible to settle a million special settlers before the end of the river navigation season, or to settle 100,000 of them during the winter." At most, the region could accept 28,000 deportees during the winter months, and 250,000 to 275,000 over the whole of the year 1933. The Committee asked Moscow to send at least 25,000 horses to Western Siberia and to see to it that the deportees arrived with at least three months' worth of supplies, as well as "a minimum number of articles for daily life, farm tools, and construction materials." It was also proposed that the head of the Siblag, Alexandr Gorchkov, go immediately to Moscow to explain in detail the region's refusal to accept a million deportees.[2]

The Siberian authorities' reaction to the massive dispatch of contingents of deportees to their region was not unprecedented. In August 1929, long before the first large-scale deportations of dekulakized peasants in early 1930, regional Party leaders in Western Siberia had vigorously protested against

the increasingly frequent dispatch of large groups of socially dangerous elements exiled to Siberia by the OGPU. We already have the burden of responsibility for 6,000 exiles and 3,000 young vagabonds who are terrorizing the peaceful population of our region, and we urgently ask an immediate halt to any further dispatch of socially dangerous elements to Siberia with-

out previous agreement on our part regarding the possibility of accepting these contingents.

Similarly, in February 1930 Robert Eikhe, who was
nonetheless a faithful Stalinist, had sought without success to "negotiate a decrease" in the number of dekulakized peasants whom the central authorities had planned
to deport to Western Siberia: fifteen thousand families
coming from Ukraine and from the central Black Earth
region, instead of thirty thousand.[3]

The regional authorities thought their area was in serious danger of being transformed into a "garbage-can
region," and that the expected benefits of a labor force
intended to exploit natural resources would be very
slight in comparison with the huge problems of policing
these enormous contingents of outlaws.

On February 10, 1933, Robert Eikhe wrote to Stalin
himself, setting forth the reasons why the plan proposed
by the OGPU's leadership seemed to him "totally unrealistic," and "thought up by comrades who know nothing
about the reality of the Great North." Eikhe emphasized
that merely in order to transport, during the winter
months, an initial contingent of 100,000 deportees to
the place assigned for their residence, along with the
minimum of supplies to allow them to survive until
summer, would require between 30,000 and 35,000
horses, far more than existed in the Narym region. Such
a mobilization could not fail to compromise irremediably
the plan for agricultural production in the whole region
for years to come.[4]

By raising this point, Eikhe, as the highest regional
party official, was making an important argument. At

this time, because of the critical situation in Ukraine and the North Caucasus, the country's two great grain-producing areas, Western Siberia, as one of the agricultural regions making large deliveries to the state, was becoming particularly strategic. In early February 1933, the 1932 plan for obligatory deliveries from Western Siberia, which should have been fulfilled by the end of the year, had still not been completed. The regional leadership had asked Moscow for a final delay until March 1. For Eikhe and the regional Communist leadership, a massive new influx of deportees would disrupt an already very precarious situation in this fragile eastern outpost of socialism.

For the past two years, Western Siberia had in fact been confronting four major problems: a serious agricultural crisis following the particularly difficult dekulakization of this frontier region, which had long before been colonized by enterprising peasants—a crisis that had led to significant shortages and even, here and there, to famines; a flare-up of ethnic tensions due to a massive influx of Kazakhs fleeing a major famine that was to kill, over the course of three years, almost a third of the Kazakh population; a sharp rise in "social disorder," and especially in outlawry in this "Far East" area where the forces of order seemed overwhelmed. The fourth problem, which will be discussed later in greater detail, was particularly difficult for the authorities: that of managing some 300,000 special settlers—chiefly peasants who had been dekulakized in 1930–31 and deported.

Western Siberia—and especially the particularly inhospitable and isolated area of Narym—received more special settlers than another other region in the USSR except the Urals.[5] Taking into account detainees in the Siblag's labor camps (about 50,000 in early 1933), and some 150,000 special settlers who had over the past two years fled their assigned places of residence, the concentration of outlaws in Western Siberia was particularly high with respect to the region's total population: more than 500,000 persons out of barely six million inhabitants very unequally distributed over an immense territory exceeding two million square kilometers in area. Thus settling under emergency conditions another contingent of one million persons seemed in fact an impossible task—even to a perfect Stalinist leader like Robert Eikhe.

Eikhe's name would probably have been forgotten like those of so many other victims of the purges of 1937–38 had the tortures to which he was subjected after his arrest as an "enemy of the people" not been discussed at length by Nikita Khrushchev in his secret report to the Soviet Communist Party's Twentieth Congress.[6] Born in 1890 in a family of farm workers laboring on the great estates of the landed aristocracy on the coast of the Baltic, Eikhe was a typical representative of the first generation of Bolsheviks. Having joined—at the age of sixteen, when he was a blacksmith's apprentice—a small social-democratic group, he rose quickly—despite being arrested and forced to flee to Great Britain and Holland—in the Latvian social-democratic party's organization, which was to become a seedbed for Bolshevik political and police officials. After the fall of the ephemeral Bolshevik power in Latvia (May 1919), Eikhe was sent, as a "commissar for supplies," to the Urals, and then to Siberia, where he displayed great revolutionary energy on the cereals front. In 1924, he was named head of the Siberian Revolutionary Committee, an authority that stood in for the Party's regular organizations in a region that was still poorly controlled by the central power. One of the chief tasks assigned to Eikhe during these years of the NEP was to break up the sales networks for the products of Siberian agriculture that were largely controlled by "nepmen"[7] and kulaks—a mission that took on very special importance for the Communist state in early 1928. Despite an excellent harvest, the peasants were grumbling about being forced to sell their products to state organs that were offering very low prices. Food supplies for the cities were threatened, and exports of cereals, which were indispensable in order to purchase the industrial equipment necessary to launch the first five-year plan, were compromised. In order to break what he called the "kulak strike," Stalin personally undertook an exceptional tour of Western Siberia. In this connection, Eikhe played a prominent role in mobilizing the support of local party officials for measures that returned to the practices of "war communism": closing markets, mass arrests of "speculators," and brutal requisitions and confiscations. It was in Western Siberia, in January and February 1928, that the NEP really came to an end. Robert Eikhe's energetic action on this occasion got him promoted, the following year, to the headship of the Party's regional organization. In this post he was the official chiefly responsible for forced collectivization and dekulakization in Siberia. Dekulakization was especially extensive in this region because there the kulaks constituted a particularly dynamic group—larger than in most other Soviet regions—within the local peasantry.[8]

The ensuing agricultural crisis corresponded to the massive repression that struck a hundred thousand Siberian peasant families summarily deprived of their land; 60 percent of them were deported from the richest agricultural districts in southern Siberia and the Altai area to the Narym region. More generally, the crisis resulted from the profound disruption of the whole mode of production, aggravated by totally disproportionate levies in the name of "state procurements" and by two years of drought.

According to official figures, Siberian livestock herds decreased by two-thirds over three years, while the grain harvest decreased by 45 percent.[9] However, the procurement plans increased by more than 30 percent over this period. In spring 1931, the OGPU's secret reports sent to the Party's regional leadership acknowledged the existence of "isolated areas of difficulty with food supplies."[10] The procurement plan for 1931, which was very ambitious (more than 1,400,000 metric tons of grain and 450,000 metric tons of meat), was fulfilled several months late and at the price of a massive slaughter of livestock and a confiscation of part of the seed reserved for the following year's harvest. In some forty agricultural districts in the southern part of Western Siberia, the shortages that appeared in 1931 developed in some places into genuine famines during the spring of 1932.

Among the many sources documenting the terrible ordeals of the Siberian peasants during these years, we will limit ourselves here to a letter written to Stalin by three Communist officials in the Berezovsky district on March 26, 1932. These officials, justifying themselves by suggesting that "given the remoteness of our area, the Central Committee is probably not aware of what is happening here":

> Since last November, more than two thousand families, that is, a fourth of the population of our agricultural district, have sold out and fled in an attempt to escape certain death from hunger. Only the congestion of the railways and the prohibition on selling tickets have allowed us to brake the flight of peasants. At the present time, our district does not have any reserves to feed starving kolkhozians.

There follows a long statistical demonstration in which the authors of the letter show that the sowing plan was completely unrealistic and that the only way out would be to send emergency food aid that would "restore the kolkhozians' confidence and prove to them that Soviet power is an authentically popular power." Accompanying the letter was a package containing physicians' and veterinarians' statements that confirmed that rotting carcasses and food substitutes, as well as wild plants and tubers, were being used to feed peasants.[11]

This step taken by Communist officials in the Berezovsky district, which was severely punished by Eikhe after he learned about it, brought the Siberian peasants no relief. The plan for obligatory deliveries assigned to Western Siberia for 1932 went beyond that for 1931. Most of the procurements were allocated for the great consuming regions of European Russia and for export. The Siberian cities scarcely benefited from the levies on local peasants. In April and May 1932, the norms for the urban population's food supply sharply decreased, leading to shortages in a certain number of cities, particularly Novosibirsk, Tomsk, Kemerovo, and Barnaul.[12]

These economic difficulties were accompanied by serious ethnic tensions aroused by the massive influx into Western Siberia of hundreds of thousands of Kazakhs fleeing the famine that was ravaging the bordering parts of Kazakhstan. Since 1930, Kazakhstan had been drawn, like the rest of the country, into the turmoil of forced collectivization and dekulakization, to which was added a vast plan of sedentarization. In this area of extensive livestock-raising and transhumance, setting up kolkhozes and sovkhozes was in fact also intended to stabilize nomadic and seminomadic breeders. At the same time, a broad plan for developing grain production was drawn up. The goal of all these measures was to move the Kazakhs from a "natural economy" to a "socialist economy" by rooting out clan structures and "feudal and semifeudal" relationships which, according to Kazakh Communist officials, were keeping the Kazakh masses in oppression.

In reality, here more than elsewhere, the race to break records of collectivization,[13] together with obligatory deliveries of meat of unprecedented levels, totally disrupted the productive cycle. The Kazakh livestock herds, which were the largest in the USSR at the end of the 1920s, decreased by more than 85 percent in three years,[14] leading to a severe impoverishment of the Kazakh population, which lived almost exclusively on livestock raising. In this situation, the nomads saw no way out but to leave. In January 1931, Stalin and Molotov were informed by Soviet consular officials in China that huge numbers of Kazakhs were migrating toward

Singkiang (Xinjiang).[15] All through 1931, the Kazakh exodus toward Western Siberia, Kyrgyz areas, and as far as the Volga increased.

The reports sent by the OGPU's secret political department to the country's leaders emphasized that most of the migrants came without their flocks, totally bereft, in an advanced state of exhaustion due to malnutrition, and were often ill and the bearers of potential epidemics. The arrival of hundreds of thousands of weakened, starving Kazakhs in regions already suffering from serious economic difficulties and even from shortages did not fail to produce many tensions with the local people, who were quick to accuse of the migrants of causing every kind of problem. The Kazakhs were suspected of spreading epidemic diseases, stealing livestock and agricultural products, eating horse carcasses, and even practicing anthropophagy. From the mining towns of Kemerovo and Stalinsk to remotest rural areas of the Altai, persistent rumors circulated to the effect that the Kazaks "stole Russian children in order to eat them."

According to very incomplete police sources, as a result of these rumors hundreds of Kazakhs were lynched in the mining districts of the Kuzbass.[16] Hundreds of other migrants suspected of theft were also lynched. This violence reflected ethnic tensions exacerbated by the hunger suffered on both sides and the resurgence of the old peasant practice of "improvised judgment" (*samosud*), in which the community itself inflicted immediate punishment on thieves and on vagabonds suspected of the worst offenses. But it also reflected the police's inability to maintain public order. In February 1932, faced with a deteriorating situation, the regional authorities in

Western Siberia decided to send the Kazakhs home. Extensive police roundups were organized, especially in cities and train stations along the rail line leading to Turksib, where most of the migrants were concentrated. Tens of thousands of Kazakhs were forced to depart in special rail convoys that unloaded their human freight in the first stations on the other side of the border between the Russian Federation and Kazakhstan. These forced repatriations led in turn to tensions between Kazakh and Siberian officials without actually resolving the situation, since many more Kazakhs continued to enter Western Siberia to escape the famine than were expelled from it.[17]

For the regional Party leadership, these interethnic tensions were only one manifestation of a far larger and more worrisome social disorder that posed a serious threat to the stability of this particularly agitated frontier area. Of all the USSR's regions, a report of the People's Commissariat of Internal Affairs acknowledged, Western Siberia was "one of those in which the situation, from the point of view of maintaining revolutionary order, is the most tense."[18] With its special settlements in the north and its anarchically growing new industrial cities in the south, together with its contingents (proportionally larger here than anywhere else) of people who were marginal, excluded, or outlaws, Western Siberia combined all the social problems. The great Siberian cities (Novosibirsk, Tomsk, Barnaul, Novokuznetzk, Kemerovo, Omsk) had the highest rates of criminality in the USSR. The record in this regard was held by Tomsk, which, according to local officials, was "totally saturated with criminals and deported elements who have fled the places of residence assigned to them."[19]

In order to combat criminality and "maintain revolutionary order," the authorities had at their disposal police forces that were notoriously inadequate (for example, there were fewer than forty police officers for Novokuznetzk, a mining city in the Kuzbass whose population had risen in three years from 30,000 to 170,000 inhabitants), poorly trained, poorly equipped, underpaid, and corrupt. In 1932, the police force for the whole region numbered no more than 2,200 men. State companies, kolkhozes, grain silos, and other strategic sites were generally guarded by more or less regular, hastily recruited militiamen whose ranks were four times more numerous than those of the police.[20] As for the political police (OGPU), in 1933 they consisted of not quite 2,000 civilian agents very unequally distributed over the region's approximately 110 districts (two-thirds of which were not served by any rail line). Whereas more than 300 agents were working in the headquarters of the Plenipotentiary Representative for Western Siberia, in Novosibirsk, no more than a dozen agents were assigned to the rural districts, including secretaries and chauffeurs.[21] This very thin network was strengthened by paramilitary detachments whose ranks varied in number (on the order of a few thousand men), deployed especially along railways, a strategic line of communication and also the site of all kinds of thefts and trafficking. The OGPU's other main sector of activity was the struggle against brigandage, a phenomenon the authorities considered particularly worrisome in the early 1930s.

A land of colonization, but also a land of exile and forced labor since the eighteenth century, Siberia had always been a place of refuge for marginal people and outlaws. After 1917, during the years of civil war, certain factors had encouraged the emergence of social banditry in this region: a peasant society in complete turmoil subjected, by both the Reds and the ephemeral White military regimes set up in Siberia, to onerous requisitions and constant conscription. At the local level, as Eric Hobsbawm has shown in his works on social banditry, unstable power in a context of shifting military fronts and frequent reversals of the situation, widespread poverty, and food shortages and famines that kindled millenarian expectations, provided a terrain that was particularly favorable to the development of "primitive rebellion."[22] During the 1918–22 period, Siberia was a crucible for all kinds of crime. Alongside bands of peasant "sedentaries" defending their territory against requisitions made by both Red and White detachments, there were also more heterogeneous "roving" bands composed of marginals, deserters, outlaws, and uprooted people en route to an improbable home or destination they had left years before. Superbly described in Boris Pasternak's *Doctor Zhivago*, these groups, sometimes consisting of hundreds of horsemen, ranged with weapons and baggage over distances as long as 800 kilometers before dissolving in the immensity of the taiga or beyond the far eastern frontier leading to Harbin, one of the main sites of Russian emigration.[23]

The end of the civil war did not put a definitive end to this kind of crime. In Siberia, it remained endemic all through the 1920s, especially in the most remote dis-

tricts where the "socially dangerous elements" were exiled and put under house arrest. In 1924, 1926, and
1927, Siberia was officially declared a "dangerous region
because of crime." A special crime-fighting commission
was set up under the OGPU's Plenipotentiary Representative, whose repressive powers were considerably
strengthened. The return in 1928 of a policy of requisitions that reminded peasants of the time of "war communism," and still more, the following year, the forced
collectivization of the countryside and dekulakization
breathed new life into rural crime. Criticizing the return
to coercion in the relationships between the state and
the peasantry, the writer Mikhail Sholokhov, in a letter
to Stalin dated June 20, 1929, reminded him that "there
is no lack of tinder for a new flare-up of crime. As the
whole history of Russia has shown, the more the state
ill-treats the peasants, the more they will resort to the
old reflex of brigandage."[24]

By the spring of 1929, rural crime was rising sharply
in the vast, poorly controlled spaces of Siberia. According to police sources, at the end of 1929 more than 450
bands of bandits were operating in Siberia. Among those
most feared by the authorities was the one headed by a
certain Koschkin that had been terrorizing the "representatives of Soviet power" ever since 1927. Called "the
black Czar" by the peasants, Koschkin, leading several
dozen bandits armed with military rifles and grenades,
was particularly attacking the kolkhozes, which he systematically burned.[25] In 1930, the police forces listed, for
Western Siberia alone, 880 such bands, while acknowl-
edging that these represented "only the groups we know
about."[26]

In an effort to halt the expansion of rural crime and to repress a peasant agitation that was in places beginning to look like genuine insurrection (the borderline between the two phenomena being indistinct), special units of the OGPU were dispatched to the most troubled districts. In the Barabinsk district alone, more than 1,000 insurgent peasants were arrested in March 1930. Of this number, a hundred, arbitrarily qualified by the authorities as "kulak criminals," were executed.[27] In an assessment of "counterrevolutionary" activities in 1930 (535 riots and mass demonstrations, 305 "terrorist acts"), the regional head of the OGPU estimated the number of active "criminals" in his area at more than 12,000. Organized in bands of several dozen individuals, the "criminals" had attacked 130 kolkhozes, making off with hundreds of horses (an important prize because it gave them great mobility, particularly in comparison with police forces that were lacking both weapons and mounts), pillaged or burned more than 200 storehouses and silos, and sacked 65 rural soviets.[28]

Crime remained endemic throughout the following years. In 1931, no less than 40 percent of the kolkhozes in Western Siberia were the victims of "attacks by criminals" or a "terrorist act" (arson, the assassination or attempted assassination of Soviet officials, Party members, and other "activists" close to the government).[29] According to police sources, these criminals were recruited primarily among kulaks who had evaded arrest and deportation, as well as among the tens of thousands of deportees who had succeeded in escaping. These "avengers" (as they called themselves) entered a very violent, criminal group whose will to settle scores with a political system that had brutally excluded and marginalized them constituted a motivation at least as strong as the desire for gain or a taste for adventure. Their primary target was local representatives of Soviet power, kolkhozes and sovkhozes, cooperative stores, depots for machines and tractors, silos in which "state procurements" were stored, and they sometimes redistributed the latter to the peasants. One of the factors stimulating this social crime that never lacked for recruits was the belief, very widely shared in these years of great upheavals, that the kolkhozian system was ephemeral: testimony to this belief is found in the countless rumors regarding the impending dissolution of the kolkhozes, the imminence of a Japanese invasion, and the regime's inevitable collapse.

To illustrate the climate of violence that prevailed in this Soviet "Far East" in the early 1930s, we will limit ourselves to quoting a passage—among many other similar ones—drawn from a report submitted by the OGPU leadership in Western Siberia, "On the Political Situation in the Region on August 15, 1931."[30] After having outlined the struggle against "insurrectional organizations and groups dismantled since the beginning of 1931 (511 groups with a total of 6,287 members), the highest regional authority of the political police went on:

> Over the past two or three months, our services have noted the hatching of a dozen new bands (144 members) as well as two major attacks (about 700 participants). . . . The breeding ground for bandits is constituted by kulaks who have evaded deportation and secondarily by criminal elements.

These bands use as bases for their activities the special villages and the most remote hamlets in distant areas of the southern part of Western Siberia that are inaccessible and covered with marshes, where the weakness, indeed the total absence, of Soviet power favors the formation of bands that recruit members among escaped kulaks, criminal elements exiled to these places, special settlers, and all those who have fled the place assigned them for residence. Nonetheless, these bands are not limited to such "wolf's lairs" in remote areas. They come down into the towns and administrative centers, where they take advantage of the excesses and errors of the Party's local organizations and soviets in order to carry on their criminal activities among the local population, particularly by spreading a whole series of subversive rumors.

These bands' criminal activities are fairly organized in nature. They often benefit from the support of the local population. Operating in the Sedelnikovo district, a band with twenty-four members, led by a certain Skuratov, killed, on July 1, in the village of Estonsky, the Communist Party member Lidia Omuk. It also fired on kolkhozians in the village of Kuprinka, burned the house of the president of the kolkhoz in Bakino, and handed out pamphlets in which it threatened to "kill all the communists and komsomols." The band recruits among escaped kulaks. Its growth can be explained by the support it enjoys among the local population (seven individuals serving as liaison agents have recently been arrested). The villagers provide the bandits with food and shelter, and keep them informed regarding our detachments' movements. . . .

According to the telegram sent June 12 by the head of the OGPU in the district of Chumakovo, a band of escaped kulaks, seventy strong and commanded by a former officer of the army of Kolchak, a certain Kalinin, has established itself in the marshy region of Ch-Mys. On July 7, this band attacked forestry workers in the neighboring sovkhoz. On July 9, it entered the village of Akininskoie, where it released a family of kulaks about to be deported. On July 10, it attacked the president of a rural soviet and two police officers who were on their way to Akininskoie to investigate the matter. The official was killed and the two police officers are reported missing. The following day, the band attacked the depot in the sovkhoz of Kreschenskoie, where it made off with sixteen *pouds*[31] of gunpowder, five rifles, and winter clothing. . . . In the town of Soyouznyi, the band has organized a "general mobilization" of the adult population against Soviet power. On July 16, it attacked our detachment at Kreschenskoia, killing three of our men. On July 18, it once again attacked our detachment, which is 150 men strong, in Dubrovskoia, but having been repulsed, it retreated. On July 19, we occupied, after fighting, Mussin-Ostrov. In the course of subsequent battles, the band has lost more than sixty men (killed), twelve wounded, and 115 have been taken prisoner. In addition, after the band was liquidated, we arrested 130 liaison agents and other bandits. The social distribution of the individuals arrested is as follows: 75 ex-

kulaks, 115 middle peasants, all of them special settlers, 37 poor peasants, 10 officials, 2 artisans, and 6
individuals whose occupations remain undetermined.
We have seized 91 firearms, 16 horses . . .

The veritable guerrilla warfare described in this report
was only the most spectacular aspect of a much larger
problem that had confronted the Party's regional authorities since 1930–31: the management of a contingent of three hundred to four hundred thousand special
settlers constituted almost exclusively of dekulakized
peasants, almost a third of which had already escaped.

In October 1931 Robert Eikhe, assessing the results of
the dekulakization program before an assembly of the
Party's high regional officers, stated that he "knew of not
a single domain in which the disconnect between the
Center and local authorities had been—and remained—as great as in the case of special settlers." The
Center had always been prompt to "manipulate statistics, elaborate grandiose development plans, and talk
about self-sufficiency in food supplies," but the funding
to do these things never followed. As for local leaders,
they had to "settle masses of people in the taiga, in record time and without adequate means, and then prevent
them from escaping."[32]

Since the beginning of 1930, Western Siberia had
been called upon to play an important role in the enterprise of "liquidating kulaks as a class," in the course of
which, in the USSR as a whole, four million peasants
were deprived of their property and 1,800,000 were deported (550,000 in 1930 and 1,250,000 in 1931). Western Siberia was in fact not only a region where rich peas-

ants were more numerous than elsewhere (they were estimated to constitute about 7 percent of the region's total population, or about 100,000 families), but also a region of colonization that had vast virgin areas that could "accept" the dekulakized deportees from other regions. In 1930–31, there were two great waves of dekulakization and deportation, making Western Siberia the region with the nation's highest relative concentration of special settlers.[33]

The first of these waves took place, in Siberia as in the rest of the country, between February and May 1930. The quotas of Siberian kulaks to be expropriated and deported to the southern part of Siberia were among the highest in the country: 30,000 families (or a fifth of the total number of families to be deported in the whole of the USSR during this first phase). In addition, Western Siberia was expected to accept 30,000 families of dekulakized persons from other regions.[34] As was the case everywhere, this first wave of dekulakization was marked by countless "excesses" and "deviations" committed by the local dekulakization committees constituted of local Communist activists, labor union members and workers sent from the cities, and poor peasants for whom the "liquidation of the kulaks as a class" was first of all an opportunity for unlimited pillaging and for settling old scores. The total expropriation of numerous kulaks raised serious problems for properly carrying out the operations of deportation. In fact, the dekulakized persons were expected to bring with them food supplies adequate for at least two months, along with the minimum in tools and materials required to settle themselves in the region, and even to provide, by furnishing one horse per family, for their own transportation from the point where the rail convoy set them down to the place of residence assigned to them.[35]

In reality, as the Party official responsible for the Tomsk region wrote to Eikhe on March 7, 1930,

> the horses assigned to the convoys are absolutely un-suited for travel over distances of three hundred kilo-meters and more, because when the convoys were formed all the good horses belonging to the deportees were replaced by nags. . . . In view of the situation, it will be very difficult to transport the belongings and supplies to which the kulaks are entitled according to the regulations, that is, for each family a total of 7 pouds of flour, 13 pouds of seed, 70 pouds of hay, 1 plow to be shared by three families, one harrow to be shared by four families, 1 fork, 2 shovels, 2 axes, 3 scythes, 1 sleigh, 1 harness, 1 saw, 2 sickles, 1 large two-man handsaw to be shared by 5 families. . . . For the transportation of bread and hay alone we would have to mobilize, in connection with obligatory public labor owed by the peasants, twenty thousand wagons, and this would seriously compromise the spring sow-ing and woodcutting plans for the whole region.[36]

Thus it was usually with very few provisions and hardly any tools that the deportees were "settled" in the places assigned to them.

How were these places chosen, and by whom? During this first phase of dekulakization, the choice of places of deportation was the responsibility of hastily set-up dis-trict commissions composed of officials drawn from the most diverse administrations: the executive committees of soviets, regrouping committees under the People's Commissariat for Agriculture, representatives of the large state forestry complexes responsible for making use of deported manpower, and OGPU directors. How could the repressive imperatives emphasized by the OGPU, which insisted that the deportees be settled "in zones whose very nature would make escape impossible (marshes and impenetrable forests), that have no roads, and are at least several hundred kilometers from any rail line,"[37] be reconciled with the economic imperatives of a "productive colonization" that was supposed to guarantee the development of the region's natural resources? These incompatible demands generally led to aberrant choices, the OGPU, which was responsible for escorting the deportees, usually having the last word.

Thus it was decided, to give a single example, to assign 11,600 deportees to the Kulaisk district, 1,400 kilometers away from Tomsk, with hardly 1,500 inhabitants, accessible from May to October by river but in winter only by rough trails. According to the report of the commission sent to inquire into the "economic use of deportees of the Kulaiskaia komandatura," 2,700 deportees never arrived at their appointed destination. How many of them died during the forty days of travel by sleigh? How many escaped? On arrival at their destination in early April, 8,891 deportees were recorded by the forty-five officials and guards specially recruited and assigned to the Kulaiskaia komandatura, an administrative entity created especially to manage special settlers. Three months later, only 1,607 remained on the site. According to the commission of inquiry, 6,682 deportees had escaped, 80 had died, and 208 had been authorized to return home.

Of the 2,254 horses that had transported the deportees (and the provisions they had been allowed to take with them), there remained only 333, the escaped dekulakized persons having left on horseback. The commission acknowledged that when the spring thaw came, the places of settlement, chosen at random in the middle of winter, had proven to be completely uninhabitable. The rough shelters constructed by the deportees themselves had been submerged; the soil could not be cultivated. The commission of inquiry concluded that the only thing left to do was to transfer the survivors to places more suitable for colonization.[38]

This case was not by any means exceptional, far from it. The number of deportees who died during the first months of settlement, as reported in this document, even appears small in relation to other data collected here and there by local officials: 200 dead, almost exclusively children, out of a contingent of 1,200 families;[39] 180 young children dead as a result of an epidemic of scarlet fever and diphtheria in a group of deportees consisting of 350 families.[40]

The almost complete disorganization, the lack of preparation of the places of settlement, the total absence of coordination among the operations of deportation carried out by the OGPU, and the settlement of deportees by overwhelmed local officials without resources—all these characterized the first wave of deportations during the winter and spring of 1930. This no doubt explains why the initial plan for deporting Siberian kulaks (30,000 families) was far from realized. Although almost 70,000 peasant families were expropriated, the regional authorities succeeded in deporting, given the deplorable condition of the roads, the lack of means of transportation, and general disorganization, no more than 16,000 families, or about 83,000 persons (among whom there were more than 38,000 children and adolescents).[41] As for the 30,000 families of kulaks from Ukraine, the North Caucasus, and the Volga regions that were supposed to be settled in Western Siberia during 1930, hardly a third of them were taken to their assigned places of residence, the rest being settled in the Urals.

The losses corresponded to the ambient chaos. In June 1930, 54,200 deportees had been settled in the Narym area; in October, there remained only 22,000. According to police sources, about 22,000 deportees had escaped. About 10,000 (18 percent!) had died, decimated by epidemics (especially malaria), exhaustion, and hunger, not counting escapees who disappeared forever in the immensity of the taiga. For Western Siberia as a whole, the OGPU listed in December 1930 100,762 special settlers; more than 42,000 were thus missing.[42] The authorities seemed particularly concerned by the fact that only a small minority of deportees were engaged in productive labor corresponding to some degree to the claimed objectives of colonizing and developing the region's natural resources. Hardly more than 4,000 deportees were working for the Siblestrest forestry complex, 3,200 for the Soyuzzoloto gold-prospecting complex, and about 2,300 working on construction of the great Kuznetzstroy metallurgical complex. The vast majority of the other deportees were trying to survive by clearing a few small tracts of land and struggling to construct rudimentary shelters.

Ultimately, the whole operation proved extremely expensive for the state. For all that, however, none of the plans for settlement, the construction of huts, or resource development had been realized. "The sums made available to the regional administration for the purpose of settling deportees in Western Siberia—a million and a half rubles," we read in an assessment report on the deportation of kulaks in 1930, "have been spent recklessly and no one knows where this money went. . . . Supplies are not properly assured anywhere, and difficulty in feeding people is developing, in some places, into genuine famines."[43] We should note that the 1,000 rubles allocated for each deported family (expenditures for transportation, management, and food supplies, no matter how minimal) was far greater than the average value of the expropriated goods, which were evaluated at about 560 rubles. Moreover, only a small part of these goods had been actually transferred to the kolkhozes, once the "dekulakization brigades" had taken their share.[44]

These considerations did not slow the pursuit of the great project of collectivization and the "liquidation of the kulaks as a class" undertaken in early 1930. Gathering in December 1930, the plenum of the Central Committee once again ratified the "leap forward" proposed by Stalin by establishing very ambitious goals for collectivization (within one year, up to 80 percent of the farms were to be collectivized in the main grain-producing regions) and by calling for the "completion of dekulakization." In an attempt to remedy the "frightful waste of labor and the disorder in making use of special settlers," the Politburo created in March 1931, just before launching the second great wave of dekulakization, a special commission led by Andrei Andreiev, the vice-president of the Council of People's Commissars, which was charged with supervising the whole of the deportation operations and setting up a "rational and effective system of management of special settlers." This commission, in which Genrikh Iagoda played a key role, considerably strengthened the OGPU's prerogatives. Whereas up to that point the political police had been responsible solely for arresting and transferring deportees, it was henceforth expected to organize their settlement and economic exploitation, which was regulated by specific contracts between the OGPU and a certain number of large complexes assigned to develop natural resources and build infrastructures in the northern and eastern parts of the country. In addition, the OGPU was given a monopoly on the administrative, financial, and economic management of the special villages that had previously been the responsibility of local authorities. For this purpose a Head Office for Special Settlements, under the Head Office of the Camps (Gulag), was created, and at the regional level, in connection with the OGPU's Plenipotentiary Representatives, Departments of Special Settlements. These latter crowned a whole network of komandaturas led by "chekist commanders" charged with administering the special labor villages.[45] The concentration of operations in the hands of a veritable parallel administration that permitted the OGPU to benefit from a sort of extraterritoriality and to gain complete control over immense territories where deportees constituted most of the local population was supposed to provide a remedy for the chaos and disorganization that had

compromised the objectives of the first wave of dekulakization.

The "second strike," as Iagoda called it, was discussed
by the Politburo on February 20, 1931. The objectives
adopted at this meeting were particularly ambitious: to
deport, within the following six months and in the
country as a whole, between 200,000 and 300,000 families (or about one to one and one-half million people)—
and let us recall that in 1930 a total of about 550,000
peasants had already been deported. The OGPU's regional offices were expected to submit, within one
month, their proposals to the Andreiev Commission,
which was responsible for coordinating the operation as
a whole.[46] On March 18, 1931, this commission discussed and approved a plan for the deportation of
40,000 Siberian kulak families that had been prepared
by the Office of the OGPU's Plenipotentiary Representative in Western Siberia, which was led by Leonid Zakovski. The operations were supposed to begin on May 10.[47]
In the meantime, the OGPU's local apparatus were expected to carefully organize all the stages in the deportation and settlement of the dekulakized people; that is,
they were to see to it that the deportees had "a minimal
number of agricultural instruments, draft animals (one
horse per family), and other production tools (hammers,
shovels, forks, saws), as well as a minimum number of
personal effects and food supplies for two months." They
were also to set up an efficient transportation system by
making use of wagons (in the framework of the obligatory public labor owed by kolkhozes) and barges for
moving the deportees by river, and to locate, "in the

context of field expeditions, places of settlement, taking into account any studies that may have been made in the 1920s by the Siberian Department of Migrations." Three million rubles were immediately allocated for these operations.[48] At the end of April, Zakovski, the OGPU's top regional official, submitted his report "On the Modalities of Settlement of 40,000 Siberian Kulak Families," a veritable masterpiece of bureaucratic planning. According to Zakovski, all eventualities had been foreseen in order to avoid the "disorder" that had characterized the preceding year's deportations. Preparations included the requisition of 33,350 wagons (in addition to 20,000 wagons provided by the dekulakized persons themselves) to transport the deportees as far as the points where they would be transferred to river boats; 450 police officers, 518 "kolkhozian activists," and 1,915 OGPU agents and guards mobilized to escort the deportees. The deportation sites had all been inspected and judged suitable for colonization.[49]

The second wave in the deportation of the kulaks of Western Siberia began on May 10, 1931 and continued until the end of August. This time, the plan's goals were not only met but even surpassed: almost 44,000 families (182,000 individuals) were in fact deported to the Narym region. Apparently the OGPU, as the sole project manager, was able to handle things more effectively. However, we should not conclude that this immense deportation took place "without excesses, deviations, or disorders," as Zakovski wrote to Moscow. Between 1,500 and 2,000 persons, chiefly young children, died during the transfers, which frequently lasted between one and two months.[50]

The reports submitted by missions carried out in the field by Ivan Dolguikh, a thirty-two-year-old chekist who had been promoted to run the regional Department of Special Settlements, describe problems just like those that had arisen during the first wave of deportations in 1930: "Most districts completely ignored the directives concerning the deportees' equipment and supplies, so that the deportees arrived in a state of advanced exhaustion"; "no fodder was provided for the horses, so that a quarter of the animals died on the way"; "the barges are too wide to navigate the Chaya and Parabel Rivers beyond their confluence with the Ob, so that it was necessary to disembark 38,000 persons at Baranovo and 25,000 at Parabel and wait two weeks before more suitable boats could take them upstream"; "the very rough directions for finding the settlement sites almost never correspond to the reality in the area"; "hardly 50 percent of the sites selected for the settlement of the deportees were able to be colonized; in other cases it was necessary to improvise and disembark elements in the wilderness." A wilderness described in these terms: "The whole basin of the Vasyugan River is an immense marshy plain cut by occasional narrow bands of earth one or two kilometers wide and five to fifteen kilometers long and covered with an impenetrable tangle of brush. No area can be cultivated without first clearing it. As for the rare meadows, they are under water until mid-July."[51]

However, such concrete, realistic remarks in field reports written during the operations of deportation totally disappeared in the triumphal assessment Dolguikh made a few months later, at the end of 1931; like the whole of the OGPU's regional leadership, he had been over-

come by a veritable colonizing euphoria. "The colonization operations in the Narym region began on May 10
and were successfully completed on June 30, 1931. We
succeeded in settling in the Narym region, which was
previously populated by only 119,942 inhabitants spread
over an immense territory of 343,984 square kilometers,
43,852 families, or 182,327 individuals, and we did so
despite great difficulties. Thus in sixty-five to seventy
days, the Narym region—which the Czarist regime had
sought in vain to colonize for three hundred and fifty
years, succeeding in settling over all that time hardly
40,000 families—has seen its population more than double. The settlement of more than 180,000 colonists radi-
cally modifies all the economic conditions in the region
and opens up extraordinary prospects for its future development."[52]

On the basis of such triumphal assessments, in late
1931 a vast "prospective plan for the development of the
Narym region" over the next two years was drawn up
and approved at the highest level in Moscow by the
Council of People's Commissars. Within two years, the
region was supposed to attain self-sufficiency in food
production, following the clearing and cultivation of
more than 110,000 hectares. The state would invest
more than 12.7 million rubles in developing the region.
In return, the special villages would deliver to the state,
starting in 1932, 2.3 million cubic meters of wood, 5,000
metric tons of fish, and "craft products" worth 16 million
rubles.

From the countless assessments drawn up in the
course of 1932 regarding the implementation of this utopian plan emerges the picture of a predictable economic

and demographic catastrophe. OGPU officials themselves recognized that "because of the complete disorder in the organization and management of labor, the work accomplished by an adult deportee never allows him to earn enough to receive the prescribed food ration." Called *paiok*, this monthly ration was theoretically—that is, when supplies had been brought in on time and in the prescribed quantity, which was far from being the usual case—nine kilos of flour for an adult worker (plus six kilos per dependent), six kilos of semolina (plus three kilos per dependent), one and one-half kilos of dried fish (plus half that amount per dependent), and 800 grams of sugar (plus 360 grams per dependent). In addition, every four months each adult worker was supposed to receive fifty grams of "ersatz tea."[53] Other foods, such as meat, dairy products, and vegetables, which the deportees were expected to produce themselves in the context of the "food self-sufficiency plan" (a halt to the importation of grains and flour into the new colonized territories was even planned for the end of 1933) were totally absent from the slim assortment composing the *paiok*.

"According to information provided by our komandaturas," wrote the head of the Siblag to Robert Eikhe on July 18, 1932,

> it can be said that the special settlers employed by the Zapsiblestrest [the largest regional forest products company] are literally starving. In the komandaturas of Parabelskaia, Mogochinskaia, and Alexandro-Vakhovskaia, the special settlers are living on roots, bark, and grass, which leads to poisoning and high mortality rates. In addition, the failure to distribute

food supplies leads to incidents (the pillaging of stor-
age areas), completely disrupts production, and en-
courages those who can still escape to do so. . . . The
housing norms are never respected; on average the
living space per person in the huts is no more than
1.5 to 2 square meters. This overcrowding is further
aggravated by the deplorable state of healthcare.
There are no medicines at all. In the Novokuzkovskaia
komandatura, about 50 percent of the special settlers
have malaria. . . . Infectious patients are not isolated.
The administration refuses to provide horses to transport the sick to the nearest dispensary, which is several dozen kilometers away. The sick and all those
who can no longer work receive no food rations.[54]

The reports submitted by the rare inspectors sent out
by the health authorities are still more precise regarding
the famine that since 1932 had been decimating the deportees in the "pioneering polygon" that the Narym region was supposed to be:

Flour, the only product that is brought in more or less
regularly, is mixed with various substitutes, particularly dried and finely ground sawdust from tree
stumps. The deportees use this mixture to make their
bread. Another substitute frequently used, especially
in the Parabelskaia and Mogochinskaia komandaturas, is birch bark. We have mentioned that in order
to satisfy their hunger as quickly as possible, special
settlers often don't even take the time to bake the
bread, eating the diluted flour as it is, mixed with water. . . . It is impossible to care for such weakened organisms in local dispensaries or even in hospitals.

Even an appropriate dietetic diet leads to fever spikes reaching 39 to 40 degrees centigrade, and at the end of four to six weeks, these exhausted patients die of paralysis of their cardiac functions. . . . For children, the situation is still more critical. In the Ketskaia komandatura, for example, both children living in orphanages and those living with their families are extremely thin. The expression on their faces, even though they are only five, six, or seven years old, is totally apathetic; these children look like old people—they hardly move, and have no desire to play. We tried to distribute as equitably as possible the 2,000 food rations for children we had been allotted.[55]

Reading these reports, we understand the causes of the terrible mortality rates among the deportees. In one year (April 1931–April 1932), in the Narym region alone, more than 25,000 people (11.7 percent) died. The authorities acknowledged that "the great majority of these deaths" was due "less to infectious diseases and epidemics, which were fairly localized, with the exception of malaria, which is endemic in the marshy expanses of Western Siberia, than to the total exhaustion of the organisms resulting from the difficulties of everyday life, the insalubrity of the settlement sites, cold, and hunger."[56] Children were the chief victims: of the 14,000 deportees who died between June and August 1931, precisely during the period corresponding to the deportation and "settlement" of the dekulakized persons, 76 percent were less than twelve years old.[57] A report submitted in January 1932 recognized that in the Narym region, mortality among children under the age of three was 8 to 12 percent . . . per month![58]

The situation was the same in the other great regions of deportation: Kazakhstan, the Urals, and the North. During 1932 alone, according to the official statistics of the Department of Special Settlements, some 90,000 special settlers died, most of them children.[59]

Remarkably, the regional authorities of the Party and the OGPU seemed far more concerned about the failure of their grandiose plans for economic development (in 1932, none of the goals set had been more than 5 to 10 percent realized), which made the system of special settlements, as Robert Eikhe said in June 1932, "an enormous burden for the regional economy," than they were about the terrifying human cost of the deportations. Commenting on the mortality rates, one high official of the OGPU wrote: "Considering the extraordinary scope of the project of colonization that has been carried out in a very short time, this level of annual losses should not be considered particularly high."[60] Far more worrisome, in the eyes of police officials, was the phenomenon of escapes—more than 47,000 escapees in one year (7,721 of which, according to police statistics, had been caught)—a phenomenon that encouraged "criminality," and more generally, what the authorities called "social disorder."[61]

At the end of 1932, the management, not only on the economic level but also on that of the maintenance of order, of some 300,000 special settlers remained, in view of the very tense situation in Western Siberia, a major unresolved problem confronting the Party leadership. We can easily understand Robert Eikhe's reaction when he learned of the new plan, hastily drawn up in Moscow by the OGPU's central leadership, for deporting a million additional people.

CHAPTER 3

Negotiations and Preparations

In his deposition before the commission of inquiry looking into the events that took place on Nazino, the head of the Siblag, Alexandr Gorchkov, summed up what happened during the mission he had carried out in Moscow in February 1933 after having received the order to settle a million special settlers in Western Siberia:

> I left for Moscow shortly after the meeting held on February 9 in the Office of the Regional Committee of the Party of Western Siberia. On arriving, I learned that it was now a question of deporting three million persons. A million to Kazakhstan, a million to someplace I don't remember, since it was planned to assign these people to a considerable number of places. The third million was for us, the Siberians. After two days of discussions, we were told that there would be two million, one million for Kazakhstan and another million for Western Siberia. At the highest level, we were ordered to draw up a complete financial and economic estimate of the cost of the operation. And to make it as cheap as possible. We drew up several different plans and submitted them to a commission of the Central Committee, and then the matter was dis-

cussed at Gosplan, where our minimal demands, those proposed by the OGPU, were once again sharply reduced. To give a concrete example: if the needs were said to be one hundred axes, seventy were requested, but the economic ministers allotted many fewer. They had probably received precise instructions that could be summed up this way: the districts could just provide the horses, means of transportation, and food supplies for three months; the special settlers could just take along their belongings, their equipment, and their tools. The funds allocated by the Center were supposed to be reduced to a minimum. When I returned to Siberia, I learned that the final figure had been reduced to 500,000 for Kazakhstan and 500,000 for us. We had to redo all the calculations, start all over again. . . . At the beginning of March, we knew that we would probably have a small proportion of déclassé elements from the cities, banished in connection with the operations of passportization. But that we would also receive criminals, repeat offenders who had been released from prison in connection with the decongestion campaign—that we didn't know at all.[1]

An enlightening deposition that shows how Stalinist political and police officials at the highest levels conceived, organized, and implemented a particular form of the "management of populations" that involved millions of individuals.

Here we will not go into the details of the monthlong negotiations conducted between representatives of the OGPU and the Gulag on the one hand, and the various economic ministries and the Gosplan on the other, under the arbitration of the two highest authorities in the country, Stalin and Molotov. On the initial plan proposed by Iagoda in early February, Stalin and Molotov had scribbled some very revealing remarks. Stalin: "A good plan, but we have to coordinate this plan with the decongestion of the prisons"; "Deport all these individuals for a period of ten years";[2] and "What has been foreseen to strengthen surveillance and prevent escapes?" As for Molotov, as a good manager of the Soviet state budget he seemed more preoccupied with the high cost of Iagoda's "grandiose plan": "The expenses—1,394 million rubles—are grossly exaggerated. The deportees themselves have to be made to pay part of the costs."[3]

After a month of hard bargaining, the deportation plan was finally reduced by half, the OGPU's central leadership having arrived at a "compromise" with regional leaders. On March 7, 1933, Eikhe sent Stalin a telegram in which he declared that he was "prepared to modify the terms of [my] earlier telegram and to agree to settle, during the spring and summer of 1933, in the districts of Narym and Tarsk, 500,000 labor colonists" (that is, twice as many as he had accepted a month earlier). This concession—which clearly shows the limits of the regional leader's "opposition" and his restricted room for maneuver in dealing with pressures from Moscow—was nevertheless accompanied by both financial demands and requests seeking to strengthen the OGPU's repressive powers in Western Siberia in the event of the feared "disorders" following the influx of so many outlaws.[4] Three days later, the Politburo approved the compromise between the OGPU and the regional leaders of

Western Siberia and Kazakhstan, and authorized the OGPU to deport in 1933 five hundred thousand persons to Kazakhstan and as many to Western Siberia.[5] A commission was set up to handle the final arbitration of the differences between the OGPU's demands and the proposals made by Gosplan and the economic ministries.[6] The whole project dealing with the "organization of labor villages" was finally adopted by the Council of the People's Commissars on April 20, 1933.[7] As the text shows, the sums allocated for the operations of deportation and settlement of the deportees were considerably reduced. The OGPU received only 251 million rubles, hardly 20 percent of the amount initially requested, 960 tractors (including 460 used ones) out of the 2,640 requested, 34,000 horses out of the 90,000 considered indispensable for transportation and the development of land cleared by the "special settlers," 12,500 cattle out of the 30,000 requested, and so on. As for seed, fodder, and other basic food products (flour, dried fish, oil, sugar, salt, tea) that had been laboriously wrung out of the State Procurement Committee, a veritable central bank for the country's food reserves, they were allocated very sparingly, at a rate of about one-quarter of the quantities initially requested. These meager supplies were, moreover, delivered several months late, in an economic situation that was, let us recall, particularly critical.

The deportation plans drawn up by the OGPU leadership and the central administration of the Gulag foresaw at this date (April 20) the following figures: 150,000 "elements" to be deported from Ukraine, 120,000 from the North Caucasus, 60,000 from Moscow and its environs,

40,000 from Leningrad and its environs, 50,000 from the Urals, 40,000 from the western region, 35,000 from the central region of the Black Earth, 35,000 from the region of the Middle Volga, 30,000 from Western Siberia, 20,000 from the region of the Lower Volga, and so on.[8]

The operations were to begin May 1. By August 15, 750,000 "elements" would be deported, and the 250,000 remaining "elements" would be deported in September and October 1933. According to the plan drawn up by the assistant head of the OGPU's Department of Transportation, I. Grach, the "optimal rate of deportation would be four daily convoys of 1,800 elements each, or 7,200 per day, 216,000 per month, two convoys a day to Western Siberia, and two to Kazakhstan, with an unloading time not to exceed three or four hours."[9] None of these "objectives" were realized. Regional officials, in a hurry to get rid of the "elements" to be deported, paid hardly any attention to the plan—the convoys set out long before May 1.

While negotiations regarding the modalities of deporting a million "elements" were being carried on at the highest level in Moscow, what preparations were being made in the field, in the isolated komandaturas of Western Siberia, for this new "operation of settling contingents" (as it was called in contemporary bureaucratic terminology)?

The whole of these operations were to be coordinated by Ivan Dolguikh, the head of the regional Department of Special Settlements, who had already supervised the great deportation of summer 1931. This young chekist leader, who came from the town of Barnaul in the Altai, had risen rapidly in the hierarchy. He had joined the

Bolshevik Party at the age of eighteen, fought in the Red Army, and, like many other Party members of his generation, had been quickly promoted during the civil war, at the end of which he had become a regimental commander. After military studies in Moscow, he chose to work for the People's Commissariat of Internal Affairs (NKVD). In 1928, he was already head of the NKVD's Administrative Department in Barnaul, before being promoted in 1931 to head the Western Siberia Department of Special Settlements, which managed more than 300,000 deportees. In his deposition before the commission of inquiry, Dolguikh referred repeatedly to the "historic and truly grandiose role" that the Party had conferred on him by naming him to this post. Certainly, he acknowledged,

> the figure of one million elements to be deported and settled—I've already frankly said this before the regional leadership of the Party, and Comrade Eikhe took due note—initially seemed to me enormous. This was the first time the Party had assigned us such a grandiose task: settling a million elements over the two or three summer months, in regions as harsh as those around Narym and Tarsk. Despite the inadequacy of our means and our managerial staff, we unhesitatingly accepted this heavy obligation, because the Party and the OGPU had ordered us to do so. . . . Could we fail, not be up to the task? The results obtained over the preceding years could only lend us confidence. I recall that Siberia has had a railway for more than twenty-five years, and during that whole time, hardly more than 100,000 colonists had been

settled between Chelyabinsk and the Pacific. Whereas in three months we succeeded in settling almost 200,000 persons in the Narym region alone![10]

Around mid-February 1933, Dolguikh sent the leaders of the thirty district komandaturas in Western Siberia a telegram announcing the implementation of a new plan for deporting a million persons, without explaining which "contingents" were involved. Each chekist-commander was to receive his "projected portion of elements to be settled," between 15,000 and 40,000, depending on the settlement capacities and the supposed resources of the various komandaturas.[11]

We will now analyze the way in which the operation was "prepared" in the Alexandro-Vakhovskaia komandatura, precisely the one that was a few months later the scene of the murderous deportation and abandonment in Nazino.

Of the thirty district komandaturas—administrative units created in 1930–31 to manage the contingents of special settlers—in Western Siberia, Alexandro-Vakhovskaia was the most northern, the largest (it extended more than 300 kilometers along the Ob River, and was about 50,000 square kilometers in area), and the most distant from the region's main urban centers. Tomsk was located over 700 kilometers, and Novosibirsk over 900 kilometers, upstream. A region of marshes and forests traversed by many tributaries of the Ob, including the Nazina River, the Alexandro-Vakhovskaia komandatura was accessible only by riverboat from May to October, when the Ob was navigable. One-fourth of the district's four thousand free citizens lived in the town of Alexandrovskoie, the seat of the komandatura. Among these inhabitants, the Ostyaks, a Siberian ethnic group that was dying out, represented about a third of the local population. Supporting themselves by fishing, picking fruit, and working in the forests, the Ostyaks led a semi-nomadic life, moving from logging areas to fruit-picking areas with their yurts and their small herds. The other two-thirds of the population were Russian colonists, farmers and forestry workers, who had settled in the region one or two generations earlier. According to official statistics, barely 30 percent of them were working in cooperatives (kolkhozes, fisheries) or state structures (forest-product companies), thus showing their legendary independence and refusal to submit to the central power.

Still more than the other districts in the Narym region, the Alexandro-Vakhovskii district, "where about 35 percent of the population was indigenous and backward," was considered as "particularly underdeveloped from the socioeconomic point of view" (as we read in a resolution passed by the local Party Committee).[12] One of the other peculiarities of this remote area was that since the 1920s it had served as a place of relegation and exile for "socially dangerous elements." At the end of 1932, the district had about eight hundred of these "elements," exiled by simple executive order, by virtue of the discretionary powers given the OGPU in this area.[13] Most of these "elements" were repeat offenders, but there were also several dozen political exiles who worked as teachers, health officers, accountants, or other "specialists" in the local administration, which was always short of trained personnel. To these "administrative exiles" (that was what this category of excluded persons was officially called) had been added thousands of dekulakized peasants deported into the Alexandro-Vakhovskii district during the second wave of dekulakization in the summer of 1931. In December 1932, 2,864 special settlers had been listed in the district: 773 men, 774 women, 1,039 children under twelve and 278 adolescents from twelve to sixteen years of age.[14] The outlaws (administrative exiles and special settlers) thus represented almost half the total population. They were spread over a dozen special villages hastily constructed by the deportees themselves. The district administration was handled by an Executive Committee of the soviets, which was in fact subordinate to the district Party Committee, led by a Communist Party member from the civil war years, Nikolay Perepelitsin, and from 1932 on, by Andrei Vlassov, who had a similar background. But in reality, since 1931 the true "boss" of the district was Dmitri Tsepkov, an OGPU official who was head of the district komandatura and thus responsible for administering the approximately 3,000 "special displaced persons" and 800 exiles deported to these particularly inhospitable places.

In a deposition regarding the events on the island of Nazino that he presented before the commission of inquiry, Tsepkov summed up his biography and career this way:

> I have been a Party member since 1924. By social origin, I am a peasant, a poor peasant, as you might expect. I was born and lived in the village of Karasevka, in the Bolotnitskii district. I served as an ordinary soldier during the imperialist war. In 1919, I returned from captivity in Germany. I rose through the follow-

ing ranks in the Party: member, and then president of the Revolutionary Committee of the village, of the rural soviet, and then president of the district Executive Committee. On May 15, 1931, I was appointed commander of the Alexandro-Vakhovskaia komandatura, which I set up. For the past two years, I have carried out all my functions as commander in full accord with regulations.[15]

Implementing an extraordinarily complex, persnickety, and usually completely inapplicable set of rules drawn up in the offices for managing special settlements—that was the constant challenge that confronted the head of the district komandatura, aided by the commanders of the "special villages." In reality, the hierarchy and the subordinates, the decision makers and the implementers, were not dupes. There existed considerable room for maneuver within the formal rules that had to be respected; as for the rest, the local officials had to avoid being caught when the Center, at regular but unpredictable intervals, decided to launch a campaign of "rectification" or denunciation of "excesses" and other "deviations."

The specific regulations that were worked out by the OGPU, and which the chekist commanders were supposed to apply, concerned both the special settlers (also called, starting in 1933, "labor colonists") and administrative exiles. Both of these groups had been deprived of their civil rights, put under house arrest, and subjected to discriminatory work conditions, either in agricultural cooperatives with a "particular status" (*vneustavnye arteli*) or in state economic complexes responsible for exploiting the natural resources of inhospitable and remote regions. Unlike administrative exiles, who were relatively few and sentenced individually by a extrajudicial authority of the OGPU, or even by an ordinary jurisdiction, to punishment by exile (which was often complemented by a term in prison or in a camp), the special settlers (or labor colonists) were deported, along with their families, by simple executive order, in connection with a political campaign launched by the central government (the dekulakization campaign, the passportization campaign for the urban population, and the campaign to "cleanse the cities of their socially harmful elements").

The archives have preserved a large number of regulatory texts produced by the managers and departments of special settlements. These documents reflect an obsessive determination to set up an orderly—and perfectly utopian—system of settlement colonies managed in a military-repressive way.

No less than sixty very detailed articles governed, for example, the countless responsibilities—simultaneously administrative, police-related, economic, financial, military, educational, ideological-political, and healthcare-related—that devolved upon the commander of a special village, a veritable potentate in his fief.[16] He was expected, in particular,

(1) "to put special settlers to productive and socially useful work, either in the framework of a contract signed with a state company, or in that of an agricultural or artisanal cooperative with a specific status." The company would be responsible, in theory, for seeing to it that the special settlers were given provisions—we've already seen what these provisions were like. The produc-

tion targets, salaries, and treatment of the deportees were "special," too. The targets were 30 to 50 percent higher than those for free workers; the salaries ludicrous and seldom paid, since the sums theoretically earned were often less than those withheld by the management to pay for the tools lent to the deportees to construct their huts, for the cost of the *paiok*, for the obligatory loan to the State, for various fees for labor unions to which the special settlers were supposed in theory to belong, and the 15 percent withheld for the OGPU![17]

(2) "to implement all the economic objectives worked out by the administrative hierarchy of the Department of Special Settlements: sowing, plowing, harvesting, clearing, woodcutting, draining of marshes, road construction, and other obligatory labor, but also "gathering berries, mushrooms, and other products, fishing and the fabrication of craft products using local raw materials," which were supposed to "contribute to the development of the region's natural resources, reeducate the special settlers through labor, and improve their everyday life";

(3) "to direct the construction of collective housing for the special settlers." Wooden huts were supposed to be constructed by the deportees themselves, in accord with the instructions in force and the absurdly detailed norms that specified, for instance, the authorized size and number of windows and stoves (two at each end of the building), the standard total dimensions (24.5 meters long and 9.4 meters wide, with a ceiling height of 3 meters, the whole structure being supposed to house ten families or fifty persons. Moreover, it was specified that each hut was to be at least 30 meters from any other structure!

(4) "to supervise health care for the population. . . .

The commander must construct one public bath for every fifteen huts, with one part reserved for men and another for women, as well as a disinfection and parasite control facility. . . . He will take all necessary steps to avoid the spread of epidemics among humans or animals and he will ensure that mothers and children are protected."

(5) "to improve the cultural, political, and educative development of the special settlers, especially the youngest. . . . The commander will do whatever is necessary to construct schools. In the absence of teachers recruited among free citizens, primary education may be provided by special settlers who have pedagogical training or can prove a sufficient degree of education. . . . The commander will organize libraries, see to it that special settlers subscribe to newspapers, disseminate the fundamental principles of Marxism-Leninism and knowledge (except for works dealing with military matters). . . . He will carry on an active struggle against hooliganism, the illegal production of alcohol, begging, prostitution, drugs, and other social deviations and anomalies."[18]

Naturally, in this inexhaustible bureaucratico-utopian literature, special attention is given to the policing and surveillance of the special settlers. Lacking a sufficient number of militiamen (one, at most, per village), the commander designated among the special settlers informants (usually one for every twelve families) responsible for reporting escapes and disturbances of the public order, and also for transmitting the deportees' complaints. A system of collective responsibility was supposed to protect this apparatus. The commander was authorized to impose fines, sentences involving labor in the general interest, or incarceration for a maximum term of one month, and, naturally, to transfer to the courts or to the OGPU all affairs considered serious. In order to limit massive escapes—repeat offenders could be sent to a camp—and to capture the dozens, indeed (on the national scale) the hundreds of thousands of escapees, rewards were paid to free citizens who helped capture escaping special settlers.

As even the top political officials, including Robert Eikhe, acknowledged, "these instructions are merely instructions. As Eikhe explained at a meeting of communist officials in October 1931,

> in reality, all that counts is how the commander operates. And in the komandaturas there are more opportunities for abuse than anywhere else. . . . In fact, with regard to special settlers, our commanders have only one fixed idea: a deportee is an enemy, a kulak; he has to be brought into line. Of course, at this point it would be false to say that the special settlers are on our side. The immense majority of them remain our enemies. But we are currently confronted by a difficult task: these enemies whom we have uprooted must now be transformed in their new environment, without giving them an opportunity to rise up against us, but by offering them an opportunity to redeem themselves through labor, to remodel themselves. That is the meaning of the decree issued in July of this year by the Central Executive Committee.[19] . . . However, our managers and commanders do not understand this twofold task: bringing into line and reeducating. . . . They think they can do whatever they like

with the enemy. We have to display in all the villages directives explaining what the commander has the right to do and what he does not have the right to do. I will give a single example among the most frequent abuses: when a special settler comes to see the commander to ask for authorization to marry, there is every likelihood that the commander will reply: I forbid you to marry such and such a person. And abuses of that kind are legion.[20]

However, the "abuses" Robert Eikhe mentions in this speech seem fairly harmless in comparison with the practices that were common in the komandaturas—without speaking of the deportees' everyday life, as we have already seen. Let us return to the Alexandro-Vakhovskii district and its komandatura, directed in 1931–32 by Party Secretary Perepelitsin and Commander Tsepkov, respectively. In a long report dated January 1932, a certain Shpek, an inspector working for the Department of Special Settlements, denounced the savage and inhuman repressive practices used in the Alexandrovskaia district. What this base-level official described was nothing less than organized hunting of human beings, in which not only local officials but also part of the local population participated. The events reported in this testimony illuminate in many respects the tragedy of Nazino, which was to take place a year and a half later, in almost the same places:

From May to October 1931, nearly 800 socially dangerous elements were exiled to the Alexandrovskaia district, which was absolutely unprepared to receive and employ such a large number of individuals, who

had arrived in addition to several thousand special settlers deported to the district at the same time. At most,
150 to 200 persons could be employed there during
the summer season. Thus the exiles brought in by boat
were simply disembarked on the banks of the Ob, not
far from the town of Alexandrovskoie, and left to their
fate, in accord with the motto "live and prosper." The
most enterprising of them, in groups of five to ten individuals, seized the local inhabitants' boats and tried
go down the Ob to reach Tobolsk. As for the others,
they remained where they were, but since they lacked
work, they naturally began stealing anything they
found to hand, so that there soon remained not a single inhabitant who had not been burgled. When the
locals sought help from the representatives of the government, the latter replied: "What do you want us to
do? There are so few of us and we are completely
powerless. Help us capture the socially dangerous elements and exterminate them." Soon these elements
started attacking the district officials themselves, going
so far as to break into the apartment of Comrade Perepelitsin, the secretary of the Party District Committee,
and steal all his clothes, trousers, and shirts. Thereupon Comrade Perepelitsin made on his own authority the decision to collect all the exiles and send them
to an island in the middle of the Ob. He mobilized all
the Communists, the komsomols, and every activist in
the town of Alexandrovskoie. . . . Once they had been
collected, the exiles were taken by motorboat to the
island and disembarked there. One must realize that
on this island there was not a single bush or the slightest little tree that could be used to make a fire. The

weather was terrible: rain, cold, frost. They were left that way, without shelter or food, for five or six days. . . . When these people were disembarked on the island, a few elements had remained near Alexandrovskoie, four or five kilometers away, and they didn't even know that they were being sought. Perepelitsin ordered us to take our weapons and shoot any we found who had not been taken away on the boats. Three komsomols, Jdanov, Sokolnikov, and Zagvozdin, went hunting. As for myself, I refused to go with them. Finding five exiles warming themselves around a fire, they shot them with hunting rifles. On the way back, they met Comrade Dokhalatov, the OGPU's local officer, and the head of the militia, who asked them: "Well, boys, was the hunting good?" Our komsomols boasted, "We shot five of them," and took them to see the bodies. "Bravo, boys," the officers said, "now get shovels and bury them," which they did without further ado.

After five or six days had passed, all the socially dangerous elements on the island were brought back and let go. Naturally, since they were starving, they immediately attacked the vegetable gardens, and started stealing all over again, and killing the livestock—in short, they terrorized the local population. As for the local administration, it did nothing. Seeing that they could count on neither the representatives of the government nor the few policemen who were supposed to maintain order, the peasants decided to deal with the problem themselves.

One night in September, I don't recall the exact date, around ten or eleven in the evening, we heard heavy gunfire that lasted a good two or three hours. I said to myself: "It's an uprising that's beginning." The next morning, I learned that it was the peasants, who had begun liquidating the socially dangerous people, and that at least eighteen bodies had been found. I myself saw four of them, and a fifth who had a deep wound from an axe, but was still alive—his name was Orekhov. . . . I can tell you that in the Alexandrov-skaia district the number of people killed was very high, for I heard that in one place three had been killed, in another four, and in still another five. Comrade Kascharine, the head of the militia, told me, asking me to keep it secret, that in the forest, near the place where people usually hunted wild ducks, about fifteen socially dangerous elements had been shot, and that all the district leaders had taken part in the execution.

Despite such savage actions, daily lynchings, cold and hunger continued to push the socially dangerous elements to commit crimes—thefts of livestock, pillaging, armed attacks. Then the local authorities decided to organize a concentration camp about 170 kilometers away from Alexandrovskoie, on the banks of the Nazina River, to isolate the socially dangerous elements there. I was made responsible for setting up this camp. I set out in search of clothing and footwear for these elements, who lacked everything. I made the rounds of all the economic organisms, obtained the necessary information, and then went to the District Committee of the Party to inform Comrade Perepelit-sin. Furious, he told me: "Comrade Shpek, you don't understand anything about the policies of our government! Do you really think that these elements have been sent here to be reeducated? No, Comrade, we have to see to it that by spring they're all dead, even if we have to be clever about it: dress them in such a way that they'll at least cut down a little wood before they die. You can see for yourself in what condition they send them to us here, disembarking them on the riverbank in rags, naked—if the government really wanted to reeducate them, it would clothe them without our help!"

I transcribe here, faithfully, the terms used by the secretary of the Party district committee, Comrade Perepelitsin.

After this conversation, I refused to organize the camp, for I had understood that they were going to send people out there and that I was supposed to see to it that they all died.

Considering what I've just said, I beg you to take the steps that are required, even if it's late.[21]

Unfortunately, we don't know how the authorities reacted to Inspector Shpek's letter. We know only that in the course of 1932 Perepelitsin was transferred within the Siblag apparatus, with the rank of "inspector," a post approximately equivalent to the one he had previously held. Rotating directors within the district was common—and so were the manhunts reported in the testimony we have just cited. In this "Far East," government officials and "activists"—members of the Party or of the Communist Youth organizations who came to the aid of the few duly-mandated representatives of the Soviet government and the forces of order—were all armed in order to cope with the attacks of "bandits." As one might expect, the dividing line between "self-defense" and bounty hunting for escapees was tenuous. "The self-defense units of the villages and kolkhozes often degenerate into groups of Red bandits," acknowledged an OGPU report, which mentioned in particular the manhunts activists had organized in August and September 1932 in the village of Tungusovo, in the Parabelskaia komandatura.[22] In the course of these hunts, some fifteen people had been killed. Among them were not only special settlers but also members of their extended families who had come to visit them. The hunter-activists divvied up the personal effects of their victims, "keeping for themselves the best-quality things, and handing over to the cooperative store the things that were worn out or poor in quality." This trafficking and the fact that some of the victims were free citizens probably explain why in this case an investigation was made.[23]

The idea, mentioned in Shpek's letter, of opening a camp in the Alexandrovskoie district in order to isolate the "socially dangerous elements" there was not, it seems, acted upon, despite the local authorities' insistent demands.[24] The leaders of the Siblag did not want to multiply the number of small concentration camps, which required numerous personnel.

In his deposition before the commission of inquiry regarding the Nazino tragedy, the commander of the Alexandro-Vakhovskaia komandatura, Tsepkov,[25] referred several times to the fact that very few even slightly reliable staff and managers had been put at his disposition to handle the situation. The personnel assigned to the district komandatura, whose headquarters were in the administrative center of Alexandrovskoie, totaled twenty-two individuals: guards, militiamen, and accountants, the intendant and managers included. An equivalent number of people, including the commanders of the special villages, were scattered throughout the district. Thus only forty-four persons were supposed to direct and supervise an immense territory of more than 50,000 square kilometers, half of whose population consisted of outlaws under house arrest. Nineteen of these forty-four persons employed in the district's komandaturas were in reality special settlers recruited into the administration because they had some competency—or simply at random.[26] One of the rare witnesses who left an account of what happened in Nazino, Ivan Ionovich Ouvarov, tells how he was recruited, at the age of eighteen, as an "assistant accountant" for the Alexandro-Vakhovskaia komandatura:

In 1930, my father, a physician in Krasnodar, decided to visit a comrade at the front with whom he had fought in the Great War, and who had settled in the province of Novosibirsk. My father wore a rather colorful travel getup, in the "Cossack" style: a fine fur-trimmed coat, a fur hat of the "Kubanka" type, and a red scarf around his neck. It was this costume that got him into trouble. Near Novosibirsk, chekists in the transportation militia forced him to get off the train on the pretext that he looked "shady." For a year, my father was moved from one prison to another, without being interrogated or charged. Finally, in 1931, he happened to be in the Tomsk transit camp at the very moment that they were sending thousands of dekulakized persons to the komandaturas in the Narym region. He was assigned, as an escorting physician, to a convoy leaving for Alexandrovskoie, with the status of a special settler. When he arrived in Alexandrovskoie, my father was finally able to write to us for the first time since his arrest. Along with my brother Stepan, we set out to find our father, hoping to convince the local authorities that they had made an error. When we got there, the commander informed us that as "members of a deportee's family," we were ourselves henceforth under house arrest, with the status of special settlers. Since I had just completed tenth grade,[27] I was named, as a person who was literate and trained in mathematics, "deputy manager, assistant to the chief accountant" of the komandatura, a certain Kisselev, who was a high-ranking chekist. As for my father, he continued to serve as a physician.[28]

This testimony reveals the extraordinary arbitrariness of the arrests made, at random, by the most diverse militias, who took away the arrested individual to be deported without the slightest indictment or judicial procedure. It also shows how the flagrant lack of "managers" allowed many deportees to enter into the administration of the special settlements. The slightest skills were welcome. Let us recall that in 1933, out of 971 persons employed in the administration of the twenty komandaturas in the Narym region, almost half (480) were special settlers.[29] Outside the administration proper, more than 500 teachers, health officers, physicians, accountants, and other "specialists," all of them deportees, were practicing their specialty in the Narym region's network of komandaturas.

How did these officials of the Alexandro-Vakhovskaia komandatura prepare themselves to "receive new contingents of special settlers" at the beginning of 1933? On February 16, Commander Tsepkov received from his superiors in Novosibirsk a telegram informing him that he was expected to "settle about 25,000 elements at the beginning of the navigation period," that is, beginning in May. In his deposition before the commission of inquiry, Tsepkov indicated that "despite this enormous and almost unreal [sic] figure, [he] immediately informed the district leadership of the Communist Party organization," and that, "by agreement with the latter, a five-person commission was appointed to search for places where the 25,000 elements in question could be settled."[30] All these officials, Tsepkov added, knew the taiga very well, being "excellent hunters." This kind of experience was indispensable, since the "komandatura had no detailed map of the region."

In a few days, the "commission" produced a "prospective plan" for settling the 25,000 "elements," dispersed over about thirty sites along four tributaries of the Ob, and within a radius of 200 kilometers around Alexandrovskoie, in conformity with instructions that specified that the "contingents should be isolated by marshy zones making any escape impossible."[31] Once the plan had been drawn up, everything remained to be done. The komandatura had no boats suitable for transporting the deportees to their "place of settlement," once they had debarked in Alexandrovskoie. The large convoys of barges transporting the deportees could navigate only the Ob. To go up the tributaries, lighter boats had to be used. The komandatura also lacked construction materials, tools, provisions, and manpower. "Three-fourths of my 3,000 deportees were already under contract with Rybtrest,[32] which was not about to let its men go," Tsepkov explained before the commission of inquiry. "As for the others, they were in no condition to work. I repeatedly asked Novosibirsk to give me enough manpower to construct even a few bakeries for bread, baths, storehouses. Comrade Gorchkov, the head of the Siblag, promised to send me support, but he did nothing. . . . I tried to sign an agreement with the Kouspromsoyouz[33] for the construction of boats, but at that time, at the beginning of March, I was called, along with all the other commanders, to Novosibirsk. I spent the whole month of March there, the trip taking more than a week one-way."[34] This was the first time since his appointment as head of the Alexandro-Vakhovskaia komandatura that Tsepkov had gone to the regional capital.

Concerning this "congress of commanders,"[35] in which some thirty district officials as well as the whole leadership of the Siblag took part, we have, in addition to Tsepkov's testimony, the depositions given by Gorchkov, the head of the Siblag, Dolguikh, the head of the Department of Special Settlements, and Makedonskii, the head of the Siblag's Department of Planning. In the course of this meeting, the commanders presented not only their "settlement plans" but also their needs and grievances with regard to equipment, transportation, food supplies, and managers for dealing with an unprecedented influx of deportees. Gorchkov acknowledged that the Siblag had received from Moscow only a tiny portion of the resources in cash and kind that had been requested for the task of settling half a million deportees. The construction of the transit camp in Tomsk, where most of the deportees were to arrive before being divided among the komandaturas of Western Siberia, was stalled for lack of funding. The persistent tensions between the komandaturas and the state organs charged with transporting the deportees (Rechtrans) and putting them to economic uses (Rybtrest, Koustpromsoyouz, Zapsiblestrest)[36] were discussed at length. Gorchkov announced that in connection with the exceptional mission entrusted by the government to the OGPU, the commanders' powers were to be considerably expanded, all the economic organs responsible for transporting and exploiting the deportees being henceforth subordinate to the OGPU, and their resources requisitioned for the settlement operations. Nonetheless, as the head of the Siblag's Planning Department, Makedonskii, emphasized, "[i]t was very difficult to organize anything at all in detail, because Moscow's plans were constantly changing: in two months we received no less than nine statistical estimates of the number of elements that were going to be sent to us."[37] In addition, no one knew exactly who these "elements" would be. "In the meeting, we were told that the new contingents would be scarcely different from the earlier ones; they would be the remaining kulaks, the same group as in the preceding years," Tsepkov said. "Hence I assumed that they would be hardworking muzhiks, bringing along their families, a few provisions, a few tools, and capable, as in 1931, of constructing in a single night a *zemlianka* for shelter, even if they were set down in the middle of the taiga. Instead, they sent me people who were alone, without family, without tools, city people who didn't know how to do anything, barefoot people without shirts or trousers."[38] In defending himself before the commission of inquiry, Tsepkov referred repeatedly to the fact that he had not been informed, or only at the last minute, regarding the "type of contingents" for which he was going to be responsible. This point was confirmed by his superiors. "In March," Gorchkov explained, "we had an inkling that a small proportion of the contingents might consist of people expelled from the cities in connection with passportization. Those elements, which among ourselves we called 'no arms–no legs,' we thought we could put them to work in some artisanal cooperative, doing sewing, for instance. That kind of activity ought to be within their competence. But that recidivist criminals would be sent to us in order to decongest the prisons—that we did not know."[39]

When he returned from Alexandrovskoie at the beginning of April, Tsepkov could not help noticing that during his absence nothing had changed. No agreement had been signed with the Koustpromsoyouz for the construction of boats, because the office responsible for food supplies had refused to release the additional rations to feed the laborers to be assigned to this task.[40] No food supply had been provided for this new influx of deportees, because "it was understood that the people would arrive with a minimum of provisions, in accord with the rules in force, that is, with food supplies for at least a month, if not for three months."

At the end of April, Tsepkov was informed by the

Siblag's leadership that he would be receiving 15,000 persons—without further specification—around the end of June, and that they would be coming from Omsk. "This telegram gave me a little relief. The leadership of the Siblag had understood that because I lacked manpower, I hadn't had time to prepare the sites. Thus I still had two good months to construct a bakery and a couple of storehouses in Alexandrovskoie, and to cut wood and prepare a stock of construction materials in anticipation of the arrival of additional deportees."[41]

A few days later, on May 5, 1933, a telegram from the leadership of the Siblag arrived, informing Tsepkov that he was soon to receive several thousand "criminal and déclassé elements."

CHAPTER 4

In the Tomsk Transit Camp

According to the OGPU and the Siblag, the masses of deportees sent to Western Siberia as part of Genrikh Iagoda's "grandiose plan" were supposed to pass through three transit camps before being transferred by river to the places of residence assigned to them. These camps were to be located at the rail convoys' main debarkation points on the periphery of the cities of Tomsk, Omsk, and Achinsk. The transit camps had been opened in 1930–31, in connection with the first two waves of dekulakization, in large open spaces between the freight stations and the rivers (the Irtysh River in Omsk; the Tom', a tributary of the Ob, in Tomsk; and the Chulym in Achinsk). Since autumn 1931, however, these camps had no longer been in use, and the hastily constructed huts had fallen into ruins. Here we will examine chiefly the Tomsk transit camp, by far the largest in the region and the one to which were sent, toward the middle of May 1933, the convoys of deportees later marooned on the island of Nazino.

On assuming his office on March 19, 1933, the head of the Tomsk transit camp, Georgi Kuznetsov, stated that the camp consisted of "a single rundown hut dating from 1930; all the other huts, half-demolished, were unsuitable for lodging anyone."[1] On March 20, Alexeiev, the OGPU's plenipoteniary representative for Western Siberia, visited the camp and ordered that within six weeks huts for 8,000 persons should be built, with 7,000 additional persons to be sheltered under tents. A sum of 172,000 rubles was allocated. It was planned that in three months (from May to July 1933), about 350,000 people would pass through the Tomsk camp, 4,000 deportees leaving every day for their final settlement site.[2]

As the Siblag's chief, Gorchkov, told Berman, the head of the Gulag, in a telegram dated April 7, "given the size of the groups to be dealt with, all the operations must be perfectly coordinated in order to avoid bottlenecks." The calendar depended on two factors: the construction of the huts, which could not be completed before May 1, and the breakup of the ice on the Siberian rivers, which, according to the data provided by the regional meteorological center, would begin toward the end of April. The convoys of deportees to be sent by river to the komandaturas could therefore begin starting May 8. Hence it was desirable that the convoys not arrive at the transit camp before the beginning of May—as was, moreover, assumed in the plan worked out by the OGPU's Department of Transportation—in order to guarantee a "fluid evacuation of the contingents." Gorchkov emphasized that "up to this point, we have not received from Moscow any precise data telling us when and where the convoys would arrive and how many persons we will have to receive in the transit camp. This prevents us from giving the Rechflot (river fleet) precise instructions regarding transportation of the special settlers. The absence of reliable and regularly received information threatens the whole deportation plan."³ A week later, the head of the Siblag sent another telegram to Berman. "Despite repeated requests," he wrote, "we have still not received information concerning the convoys, the length of time involved, the dates of arrival, the number of contingents, or the equipment and provisions that will have to be transported along with the contingents. We have still not received the program authorizations and government vouchers for the 20,000 metric tons of grain reserved for the first installment of the operations. The second installment of 20,000 metric tons has thus far been neither programmed nor reserved. Concerning the other products, the situation is the same. . . . This threatens to totally destroy the transportation plan that our services and the Rechflot worked so hard to put together. Moreover, the absence of funds, provisions, and budget authorizations does not allow our commanders to make satisfactory preparations for receiving the deportees at their final settlement sites."⁴

In the meantime, beginning on April 9, the first convoys of deportees began flooding into the Tomsk transit camp. The construction of the huts was far from finished, a food supply system for the camp had not yet been organized, and no "dispatch to the final settlement sites" could for the time being take place, since the rivers were not yet navigable. In three weeks, from April 9 to April 30, more than 25,000 deportees were set down at Tomsk, coming from Ukraine, the North Caucasus, the Volga regions, the resorts on the Black Sea, and from Moscow and Leningrad.⁵ According to the camp authorities, three-fourths of the deportees were "rural elements, kulaks, individual peasants, and kolkhozians who had been sabotaging the construction of collectivized farming," the rest consisting of "criminal elements and déclassés from the cities."

However, local and regional officials' reports regarding the "state of the contingents" coming from Ukraine, the North Caucasus, and the Volga regions, all of which were ravaged by famine, point to a very different reality: most of the deportees were starving peasants who had been loaded up and sent off in haste, and who on arrival were no more than "semicadavers."[6]

"The information at our disposal regarding the state of health of the contingents disembarked at Tomsk and Omsk between April 18 and May 14," the head of the Siblag reported to Moscow,

> continues to be alarming. The convoys were sent without the slightest consultation or planning.[7] They consist, in the immense majority, of individuals who have lost a great deal of weight and are suffering from acute gastrointestinal problems. We have already seen a certain number of cases of typhus. On the way, the contingents rarely received any hot meals. There was no boiled water. At the embarkation points, the contingents were not subjected to thorough hygienic measures, which explains the enormous parasite and lice infestations with which they arrived. In general, the whole organization of the transfers, from the outset and along the way, was defective. For example, to the convoy that left Bataisk (North Caucasus) on April 14, headed for Tomsk, 200 detainees were added in Sochi, in the context of the campaign to decongest the

prisons. Upon leaving, the latter were given bread sufficient for a two-week trip, at a rate of 400 grams a day. Naturally, this food was completely consumed during the first three days, so that for the rest of the trip, these people had nothing more to eat. They arrived in Tomsk in an advanced state of emaciation. Of the deportees put in the convoy that arrived in Tomsk on May 6, coming from Kushevka (Middle Volga), 80 percent were already emaciated when they got on the train. Half the people who arrived at the destination point in the previously mentioned convoy looked like semicadavers, and the vast majority of them had to be immediately hospitalized.[8]

An eloquent testimony that is confirmed by numerous other bureaucratic sources, especially the convoys' "logs," which often included these four minimal elements: the number of deportees loaded, the number of deaths en route, the percentage of individuals who had lost large amounts of weight, and the percentage of individuals infested with lice. In convoy no. 24, which departed from Bataisk and arrived in Tomsk on April 30, there were sixty-two deaths during the ten-day trip; "on arrival, the great majority (90 percent) were emaciated, having received no more than 300 grams of bread a day during the trip . . . and having no personal provisions."[9] In another convoy, which also arrived on May 6 from Bataisk, one of the main embarkation points for the convoys of peasants deported from the North Caucasus, there were sixty-nine deaths en route, and more than four hundred "semicadavers" on arrival.[10] In the convoy coming from Ritischevo (Middle Volga) that arrived on April 20, there were seventy-eight deaths en route, and "100 percent were lice-ridden, as a result of a total absence of hygienic measures at the point of departure."[11] According to a check made regarding five convoys totaling 10,185 deportees from the North Caucasus, there were 341 deaths en route, or 3.3 percent.[12] As we will see later, these numerical data extracted from a few of the convoys' "logs" were very succinct, frequently incomplete, and often nonexistent. They only partially reflected reality.

For the local authorities, the arrival of the convoys raised three immediate problems: What should they do with the "semicadavers," since the transit camp was still under construction and had only a single, rudimentary infirmary with only about forty beds? How could an explosive epidemic of typhus be avoided? More generally, how could they manage the forced transit, over a period of several weeks, of a number of deportees five to six times greater than the camp's capacity?

According to the statistics provided by the Tomsk transit camp's administration, in the second half of April more than 500 deportees died in the camp during the days following their arrival. In the course of the next two months (May and June 1933), another 1,700 deportees died, the great majority of them "as a result of a general weakening of the organism." According to the same source, out of a total of 40,698 deportees, 11,788 were listed as "ill" and received medical attention in the "Siblag's health care structures established in the Tomsk transit camp"[13] A figure that seems doubtful, given what we know about the camp's "health care structures."

To everyone's surprise and relief, the much-feared typhus epidemic did not occur, despite the terrible hygienic conditions and the overcrowding of deportees in squalid huts. A few dozen suspected cases of typhus were promptly quarantined. But the threat remained, and despite the risk that the disease would spread the moment the emaciated and weakened deportees were sent out to the remote komandaturas in the Narym region, the local authorities constantly called for their immediate departure and the closing of the transit camp.

In his deposition before the commission of inquiry, Gorchkov referred to the "panic" that overcame the Tomsk authorities when the convoys of "starving and contagious" deportees arrived at the city's gates:

> The Party's and the soviets' organizations truly panicked. It has to be granted that the convoys arrived in a terrible state. I have here reports on the hygienic situation that I can show you. The figures are in fact alarming. All of us—not only the Office of the Plenipotentiary Representative but also the Party Regional Committee, the regional Executive Committee of the soviets, the city's Party Committee—sent signals; we complained about the state in which these people had been sent to us. Moscow's only reply was to urge us to be firm, calm, to avoid upsetting the population, and to put a stop to rumors. That was not enough to reassure the Party's organizations, the soviets, and the komsomols, who had literally panicked. It has to be admitted that typhus posed a serious threat. I served in the army, and I know that if there are cases of typhus in a convoy, you have to immediately quarantine them for twenty-one days. I immediately went to see the Plenipoteniary Representative. The Polpred[14]

replied, "You have to send them away immediately, as far as possible; new convoys are arriving every day." I went to see the head of the regional Executive Committee, Comrade Reschikov, and asked him, "Do you think we can send out all these people in the condition they're in, when more than 50 to 60 percent of them are infested with lice?" The same response from Reschikov: "Send out all these elements as soon as possible. We have to get them out of town. We have to free Tomsk!"[15]

In the meantime, things had come to a standstill: the rivers were not navigable and the barges promised by the Rechflot were unavailable, but the convoys were coming in with increasing frequency—one on April 9, two on April 11, two on April 20, three on April 24, two on April 27, two on April 29, two on April 30. The chaos caused by this concentration of more than 25,000 deportees under very precarious conditions was further aggravated by a telegram from Genrikh Iagoda, dated May 2, ordering that a "detailed check" be made of the five convoys that had arrived during the last days of April from the resort areas on the Black Sea, Sochi and Tuapse, as well as from the Caucasian spas of Mineralnye Vody and Kislovodsk. Iagoda wrote that information he had received suggested that the cleansing operations in these cities had not been conducted "in conformity with the instructions given."[16] Let us recall here that on April 4, the Politburo had adopted, in connection with the general deportation plan, a specific resolution ordering "the expulsion and immediate deportation, within ten days, from the districts of Sochi, Tuapse, and Mineralnye

Vody, of 5,000 families of counterrevolutionary, parasitic, and déclassé elements who are polluting these resort areas."[17] This order had been rapidly carried out. On April 15, eight convoys carrying a total of 12,214 persons were already on their way to Western Siberia, five of them going to Tomsk, and three to Omsk and Achinsk.[18] Too rapidly, no doubt. The OGPU leadership was informed of numerous "excesses" and other "deviations" committed by the authorities in the resort areas, possibly following complaints sent in by relatives of persons who had been unjustly deported, among whom there were a certain number of Party members. It has not been possible to reconstruct the precise reasons why the head of the OGPU decided to have convoys fifteen through nineteen arriving in Tomsk checked, and only those. Nonetheless, the verification of the bases for the deportation of some 6,500 persons began on May 6 and lasted more than three weeks. On May 16, Alexeiev, the OGPU's Plenipotentiary Representative for Western Siberia, sent Iagoda a long memo detailing the first results of the inquiry.[18] The latter, he said, had revealed "an incredible number of cases of negligence and abuse."

Like a good official, Alexeiev blamed first of all the "administration's execrable handling of the files and of the whole of the prescribed procedures":

The convoys coming in from Tuapse arrived in Tomsk without regulation documents: no personal dossiers on the deportees, no lists of names, no data making it possible to understand the reasons that had led to this or that person's being deported. The convoy from Sochi arrived with lists that were not signed by the authority certifying the documents. These very in-complete lists, which covered scarcely one-third of the total number of deportees, included many names that had been struck through, and the rubric "reason for deportation" was missing for about 40 percent of the names listed. The convoys coming from Piatigorsk and Kislovodsk arrived without the prescribed documents: at most a few illegible lists scribbled in pencil on poor-quality wrapping paper. These lists had not been certi-fied by any authority whatever. On the basis of such documents, it was naturally impossible to determine with precision how many individuals had been put in the convoy, and how many had escaped or died en route.[20]

This is an important remark that requires us to view with a certain skepticism the figures quoted above re-garding the number of deportees who died during trans-fer. Most of the deportees, Alexeiev went on,

arrived without provisions or personal effects. Con-trary to the instructions given on this subject, numer-ous individuals who had apparently been rounded up at random in markets, train stations, and on the streets had been given neither the authorization nor the time to take indispensable things and provisions from their residences and arrived with only what they had on them at the time they were arrested.

At the end of ten days of hearings, the commission set up to verify the basis for the deportations had estab-lished that about 20 percent of the deportees whose cases had been examined—that is, 640 persons—were "individuals completely unsuited for labor—old, invalid, simpleminded, or blind."[21] Most of these deportees (480 out of 640) were between fifty and sixty years old, but there were 109 between sixty and seventy, 32 between seventy and eighty, and 19 between eighty and one hundred!

So many elderly people, usually alone and invalids, could be explained, the head of the OGPU concluded, only by the practice of massive roundups carried out not only in public places such as train stations and markets, but also in hospices, with a view to "relieving themselves of burdens by sending them as far away as possible." The memo Alexeviev sent Iagoda included an unusual appendix: a whole album of photographs taken in the Tomsk transit camp, showing invalids and decrepit old people who had been deported from the cities of Sochi, Tuapse, Piatigorsk, Kislovodsk, and Mineralnye Vody. Some of the most emblematic cases mentioned in the file and summed up in a few short annotations or explanations accompanying the photographs are the following:

Mark Perevalov, 103, "deported in the convoy from Piatigorsk. It proved impossible to determine his biography and the circumstances in which he had been taken away. Unable to stand up. Completely decrepit. Does not speak." (Photo)

Evdokia Kotelnikova, 85, "without family, cannot stand up, half-naked, bedridden. A decomposing semi-cadaver. Unable to speak or move. (Photo)

Elizabeta Zolotareva, 85, "without family, unable to move about on her own. Was expelled from Kislovodsk on the pretext that she was the former owner of a factory and a prostitute." (Photo)

Tatiana Staritskaia, 78, without family, "expelled from Sochi as the owner of a revenue-producing building and a person with income not derived from labor." (Photo)

Matriona Eremenko, 71, "deported from Tuapse as a parasitical element; invalid unable to walk."

Nina Kirch, 74, "invalid deported from Sochi with her son, who is mentally retarded and completely dependent."

Grigorii Chikov, 53, "blind, a beggar. Says he comes from a family of poor peasants, deported from the spa town of Essentuki as a parasitical element." (Photo)

Alexei Ostrovenko, 69, "invalid, expelled from Piatogorsk with his wife, also an invalid. Says he works as a caretaker. He and his wife can move about only on crutches." (Photo)

Elizaveta Chelepova, 91, "invalid, deported from Mineralnye Vody with her daughter, aged 63, also an invalid. Reason: ex-merchant who had always lived on income derived from the exploitation of others." (Photo)

Iouvelina Pelefalian, 75, "deported from Sochi with her deaf-mute son. Reason: merchant, living on in-

come derived from the sale of milk from her cow."
(Photo). Deported with a neighbor who shared the
same room in a communal apartment. The neighbor
was mistaken for a member of her family.

Miron Korotenko, 76, and his wife, 75, "deported
from Mineralnye Vody, 90 percent invalid. Reason:
deprived of their civil rights, simulator-parasites refusing to work on the collective farm." (Photo)

This already long list could be extended. Under the
rubric "reason for deportation," filled out in haste by the
same police officials who had carried out the operations,
we find frequently repeated, in order to "justify" the
brutal expulsion of invalids and useless individuals "polluting" (as contemporary terminology put it) the resorts,
a certain number of clichés: "parasitism," "income
drawn from an activity not related to labor," membership in the category of "people of the past" (former landlords, persons of independent means, officials of the
Czarist regime, etc.).[22]

The OGPU's Plenipotentiary Representative for Western Siberia designated another group of "several hundred persons who were abusively deported by officials
in the course of random roundups that had no objective
other than to fulfill quotas and to relieve themselves as
quickly as possible of a task imposed on them or that
arose from unverified denunciations." There followed a
long list of cases presented as particularly characteristic:

M. Arofimovich, 32, "deported with his wife and
nine-year-old daughter because he had sold tobacco
illegally in 1931."

Andrei Alexeienko, 57, "ace mechanic-worker deported from Sochi because he had his own house, and in the past had owned a small bookstore."

Dimitri Chintiapkin, 44, "manual laborer who came to Tuapse from Central Asia. Intended to take his family back to Central Asia, was picked up when doing errands in the market, taken directly to the convoy and deported without his family."

Piotr Tsal', 51, "tailor, deported from Sochi. His daughter and son-in-law are Party members and are in the diplomatic service abroad. Deported because he owned his house."

M. Livchits, 62, "retired, deported from Sochi. Taught mathematics for thirty-seven years. One of his sons is an engineer in Leningrad and a Party member. The other son is a teacher of mathematics. Deported as a parasitical element."

Maria Lavrikova, 35, "waitress in the Riviera Hotel in Sochi. According to her statements, her husband is a battalion commander in Amur province, and holds two Red Flag decorations. Deported with her father, aged 71, her mother, aged 70, and a brother, aged 22. Reasons unknown."

N. Khavadegia, 45, "deported from Sochi without reason. Her husband is a Party member, card no. 1646240. At the time of the roundup, she was carrying out a mission for the Central Committee of the Communist Party of Georgia."

A. Popova, 30, "arrested in the Tuapse train station, where she had gone to meet her niece. A. Popova works in the port and cannot in any way be considered a parasitical element."

Natalia Barabanova, "arrested during a roundup in the Sochi market, and immediately put in a departing convoy. N. Barabanova is married to a dock worker. All her requests to be allowed to go home, to notify her husband, to take along three children, including an infant, were refused. Several weeks after her arrest, no one in her family knows what has happened to her. The reasons for her arrest are unknown. After considering all hypotheses, Barabanova thinks she was arrested for having bought a kilo of dolphin fat from a shady character in the market."

Evguenia Markovkina, 18, "deported from Tuapse with her sister, 17, and her two brothers, 13 and 5, because her father, who died in 1931, had been a shady operator in the past. The five-year-old died en route. Since no one was authorized to leave the convoy, the boy's body was thrown out the window."

Vera Mirochnichenko, "Party member, card no. 1471366. Rounded up and deported when she went to get things from the apartment of her ex-husband, who was about to be deported as a déclassé element. Despite her protests, Mirochnichenko was put on a convoy along with her husband, and was not authorized to return to her home in order to prove her identity and her membership in the Party."

Of the thirty-odd examples cited, only the last one bore in the margin an annotation scribbled in pencil by the head of the OGPU: a double exclamation mark, followed by a question mark.[23] Why did this particular case attract Iagoda's attention? What was so scandalous about it? Probably just one thing: in this long list of abuses, it was the only case directly involving a Party member.

In the minds of the political officials responsible, where was the dividing line between deportations that were "abusive" and those that were not, in view of the fact that the "categories" targeted and subject to expulsion—"counterrevolutionary, parasitic, and déclassé elements"—were extremely fluid? It is impossible to know, exactly, insofar as the inspectors who had checked the convoys gave no specific examples *a contrario* of expulsions considered "in conformity" with the directives. Two kinds of expulsion and deportation were nevertheless considered "abusive": those involving people who were too old to work or infirm, and thus represented so many "useless mouths to feed" and "burdens" for which the Department of Special Settlements was henceforth responsible, and those that involved individuals considered "socially close to the Soviet government"—workers, Party members, or a Communist's family members.

At the end of his report, Alexeiev estimated at 928 the—provisional—number of families and single persons[24] deported "in violation of instructions." A considerable number, given that at the time the report was written, only a portion of the 6,500 persons transported in the five convoys coming from the resorts on the Black Sea and the spa towns of the Caucasus had been checked. A month later, in the final report, it appeared that of the 6,463 deportees "checked," 51 percent had been released after it turned out that they had been unjustly expelled. Released, but without the right to return home, and also with a prohibition on settling in a dozen cities (such as Moscow, Leningrad, Kiev, Odessa, etc.) "subject to special rules."[25] Moreover, the head of the Siblag explained that 375 persons belonging to the "checked" contingents, most of them invalids and elderly people, had died in "the Siblag hospital in the Tomsk camp."[26] Unfortunately, we do not know the ultimate fate of the deportees "released" from the camp. What happened to them? Did they defy the prohibition on going home? Did they try to make a new life in Siberia? One thing is certain: they increased still further the massive numbers of the "elements" who were uprooted, marginalized, and suspected for the sole reason that they had been caught, rightly or wrongly, in the nets of the police.

Before the commission of inquiry, Kuznetsov, the head of the Tomsk transit camp, explained how much the "checking," carried out over several weeks, of the convoys coming from the resort towns of the Caucasus had contributed to the "organizational chaos" and "congestion" of the camp at the very time that another category of contingents was flooding in—the "déclassé elements" from Moscow and Leningrad, the very "elements" who were to be sent, in haste and without "adequate preparation," to the most remote and most inhospitable of Western Siberia's komandaturas, that of Alexandro-Vakhovskaia.

The first convoy, consisting entirely of prisoners sentenced to terms of less than five years and deported as "work colonists" in connection with the campaign to "decongest the places of detention," arrived from Moscow on April 18, with 635 persons.[27] It was followed by four additional convoys: one from Leningrad, which arrived at the camp on April 20, another from Moscow, which arrived on April 27, and two further convoys that arrived in Tomsk on May 10, 1933; one of the latter had left Leningrad on April 29, and the other had left Moscow on April 30.[28] In three weeks, the transit camp, which was already saturated, received more than 6,000 "déclassé elements." Under this rubric, the authorities combined two very different categories: common criminals who had already been sentenced and who had been transferred directly from prison, and "parasitic elements, vagabonds, and beggars living illegally, polluting Moscow and Leningrad," and who had been arrested in police roundups and deported as part of the passportization campaign. According to the plan drawn up by the OGPU, in the course of 1933 about 60,000 déclassé elements were supposed to be deported from Moscow, and 40,000 from Leningrad.[29] The approximately 8,000 persons who arrived in Western Siberia (about 6,000 in Tomsk and 2,000 in Omsk) starting in the second half of April ("ahead of schedule" according to the deportation plan, which was supposed to begin on May 1), constituted in reality the first contingents of a vast operation intended to "decongest" the prisons and "cleanse" the cities—and first of all the cities "subject to special rules." As we have already seen, this operation itself represented only one part of the "grandiose plan" of deportation worked out by the OGPU leadership in February 1933.

The influx, both earlier and much larger than expected, of these urban déclassé elements at once aroused the greatest concern among the OGPU's Siberian officials. On May 3, Gorchkov sent a telegram to the head of the Gulag, Matvei Berman, in which he expressed the gravest doubts concerning the possibility of adapting and reeducating the "urban déclassé elements" who had been sent as work colonists to the remote komandaturas of Western Siberia. It was an illusion, Gorchkov explained, to think that the same treatment could be applied to kulaks who were used to managing for themselves in a hostile natural environment and to "déclassé urban elements" who had "no inclination for work, not to mention agricultural development or woodcutting." Sending these individuals to special villages, thus putting them in contact with "former contingents of special settlers" and the local population, would inevitably result in serious incidents.[30] The head of the Siblag later stated that at the beginning of May he had proposed to Moscow a solution that had not been adopted: sending the strongest part of the contingents of déclassé elements, estimated at about 25 percent of the total, directly to a work camp and releasing all the others.[31] For his part, the OGPU's Plenipotentiary Representative for Western Siberia had advanced another "solution," which was also rejected, but which clearly shows the regional officials' perplexity when forced to deal with such a large number of déclassé elements that socialism's display-window capital cities were getting rid of. In a long telegram sent on May 15 to Genrikh Iagoda, Alexeiev wrote:

As of today, we have received 7,985 urban déclassé
and socially harmful elements, consisting chiefly (92
percent) of men, most of them under the age of thirty,
very poorly clothed and shod, lacking any skills or
taste for work, and often suffering from syphilis. I em-
phasize that putting this contingent to work within
the usual structures, namely the special-status cooperatives, or even on individual farms—which would
presuppose the granting of loans and means of production—does not in any way guarantee a return on
investment. To avoid massive escapes and in order to
keep déclassé and socially harmful elements from disturbing the local population and work colonists who
have already been settled, we are sending these elements to the most distant northern districts, distribut-
ing them over specific sites, and bringing in additional
guard and supervisory personnel from districts that
present no particular problems. In my view, it is indispensable to establish a special set of rules for the déclassés and socially harmful elements that is different
from that for the other work colonists. We could try
the solution of the OGPU's labor communes.[32] In any
event, considering the great difficulties involved in agricultural development in Western Siberia and the total unsuitability of déclassé elements for this undertaking, I urgently ask that you no longer send us this
type of contingent. Telegraph your decision on all the
points raised in my dispatch.[33]

Moscow did not reply for two weeks. Finally, on May
27, the head of the Gulag sent the following telegraph
to Novosibirsk:

There are no plans to send you further contingents of déclassés. I repeat, there are no plans to send you this type of element. We approve your proposals to settle these contingents in remote, isolated districts. . . . You will probably have to see to it that camps are rapidly set up and that the déclassés and socially harmful elements are put in them. The solution of work communes does not seem to us appropriate.[34]

These exchanges between the Gulag's highest officials clearly show that no one knew exactly what to do with the "déclassés and socially harmful elements." In the interim, this type of contingent continued to be sent. On June 17, a convoy of 1,754 déclassé elements that had left Moscow on June 6 arrived in the Tomsk camp. In the confusion surrounding its arrival, 204 persons escaped.[35] The regional officials responded a few days later by sending a new telegram, signed jointly by Gorchkov and Alexeiev and sent to the head of the Gulag in Moscow:

Contrary to all the assurances given earlier regarding a halt to the deportation of déclassé elements, and also contrary to the information received . . . we continue to receive essentially individuals without families, déclassés, and recidivist criminals. In the course of June alone, after your telegram of May 27, we received from Moscow a further 5,680 individuals, 3,744 of them without families, and most of them recidivists. The plan we had worked out on the basis of the information regarding the sending of families must be entirely revised. The unexpected, unprogrammed influx of a mass of déclassé elements and recidivists puts the whole plan for developing our region at risk. . . . We urgently ask you, once again, not to send us any more of these contingents.[36]

In turn, the "boss" of the region, Robert Eikhe, protested to the Politburo, asking both that increased repressive powers be granted in order to "struggle against criminal elements terrorizing the local population" and that the deportation of déclassé elements to Western Siberia be halted.[37] Stalin demanded explanations from Genrikh Iagoda. The head of the OGPU replied that

in fact, as of today, about 17,000 déclassé elements have been sent from Moscow and Leningrad to Western Siberia and the Narym region in particular. The OGPU's Plenipotentiary Representative has chosen to settle these elements in the most remote and isolated district of the region, that of Alexandro-Vakhovskaia, which extends as far as a thousand kilometers from Tomsk, and to subject them to increased surveillance while awaiting the imminent opening of camps. This is a correct decision. . . . It is not desirable to stop sending déclassé elements from cities subject to special rules, since we will certainly not find any place in the country more suitable for these people than the Alexandro-Vakhovskaia komandatura.[38]

At the moment the head of the OGPU was writing these lines, word of what had happened on the island of Nazino—an "incident" that local officials had tried to hush up—had just arrived in the head office of the OGPU's Plenipotentiary Representative for Western Siberia, but not yet in Moscow.

Let us return to the convoys of "déclassé and socially harmful elements" that arrived from Moscow and Leningrad in the Tomsk transit camp during the second half of April and the beginning of May, 1933—and that were to be sent, starting May 14, to the Alexandro-Vakhovskaia komandatura. Who were these "elements"? In what circumstances had they been arrested and then sent to Tomsk?

In reality, we have very little reliable, precise information about these people. And there is a reason for that. As the head office of the Siblag emphasized in a telegram sent on April 25 to Zaporojets, the OGPU's Plenipotentiary Representative for the Leningrad region,

> Convoy no. 744 coming from Leningrad arrived in total violation of directive no. 042–33 regarding procedures for transporting persons sent to special labor villages. None of the deportees had a personal file. No document or extract from a decision explaining why they were sent to a special labor village. A few very incomplete lists, with neither signature nor the seal of any authority whatever. Moreover, you did not inform the Siblag of either the date of departure, the number of individuals sent, or the composition of the convoy (single persons or persons with families).[39]

This kind of "violation of procedures"—as we have already seen with respect to the convoys coming from the Black Sea resort towns—was very common, occurring repeatedly, in particular in the case of convoys of déclassé elements sent hastily from Moscow. In his deposition before the commission of inquiry, the head of the Tomsk transit camp reported:

Only a small proportion of the family names that we were able to decipher on very incomplete lists scribbled in pencil corresponded to the actual persons. It has also to be said that the déclassé elements from Moscow did their best to confuse matters. Every one of them had twenty different names, and as many nicknames. Nobody responded to the roll call. When the convoys arrived at the camp, and when they were sent on to the komandatura, we could do no more than count and recount them. No files, no certified documents, no papers, and family names that were constantly changing. If they escaped, we couldn't even write a proper report, because we didn't know the fugitive's family name.[40]

For Dolguikh, the head of the Siblag's Department of Special Settlements, these anonymous deportees formed an undifferentiated mass, which they described in these terms: "The contingent that was sent to Nazino consists of the rejects of society, the most déclassé and most socially harmful elements in the cities, criminals and delinquents who stop at nothing: stealing, pillaging, killing."[41] However, most of the OGPU's other officials who had dealt with this "contingent" distinguished within it three different categories of individuals. About one-third of them were seen as "hardened criminals," and half as vagabonds, beggars, petty delinquents, ruffians, hooligans, or other marginal types whom a Siblag inspector described as "street people, without fixed domicile, accustomed to beg, engage in petty schemes, speculate, steal, and in short live like parasites on others, without the slightest desire to work or to integrate themselves into our new socialist society."[42] The third category (estimated at about 15 percent) consisted, as even the chekists admitted, of individuals "rounded up and deported by chance"—Kolkhozians or seasonal workers who had come to get supplies or look for work in the capital, as well as native-born residents of Moscow and Leningrad who had been arrested and immediately expelled because they weren't carrying their passports on them.

In reality, it was only in the course of the inquiry that Vassilii Arsenievich Velichko, a journalist-propagandist with the Party Committee of the Narym region and a journalist, conducted almost three months after the deportation and abandonment of more than 6,000 déclassé elements on the island of Nazino, that a few names, a few testimonies, a few individual stories began to emerge from the faceless mass of the deportees. Only after Velichko sent Stalin a long letter relating what had happened in Nazino was a commission of inquiry, led by Maxim Kovalev, a high regional Party official, finally set up in mid-September 1933—four months after the events. This commission's members were sent to the site to collect depositions from the responsible Siblag officials in order to shed light on the sequences of events that had led to this particularly murderous deportation-abandonment, to establish who was blame for what, and also to determine the validity of the claims of hundreds of survivors who said they had been wrongly deported. No matter how incomplete they were, the inquiries conducted by Velichko and by the Kovalev Commission enable us to reconstruct a rough outline of the main categories of individuals who were arrested in the roundups and deportations that occurred in Moscow and Leningrad at the end of April 1933, the specific circumstances in which these expulsions took place, and how things were done in an environment characterized by an absence of law and by arbitrary police action.

A first set of deportees—about 3,000 persons out of some 8,000 put on a convoy headed for Western Siberia—did in fact consist of detainees who had been arrested and sentenced over the preceding months to terms varying from one to five years in a camp. More than "hardened criminals," as Siblag officials called them, they were mere petty delinquents, who, although young (the majority were between sixteen and thirty years old), had often committed more than one offense, and had been convicted mainly of theft, hooliganism, "speculation" (that is, the resale of products in short supply), receiving stolen goods, and other kinds of petty trafficking. The sharp increase in the number of convictions since the summer of 1932, along with the lengthening of prison terms, had contributed to the "congestion" of the prisons and penitentiary colonies to which detainees serving short terms were usually sent. Hence the idea of transferring large numbers of the latter to labor villages.

A second and more numerous set of deportees consisted of individuals who had been rounded up by the police for having violated the new passport regulations and the law concerning residence in cities "subject to special rules." Particular targets were homeless persons, beggars, vagabonds, and other "déclassé and socially harmful elements"—a group whose contours were, as we have seen, vague and fluid. Nevertheless, as is shown by the fifty-two examples of "abusive and unjustified deportation" that the journalist-propagandist Velichko and the Kovalev Commission mentioned, among hundreds of others, as being "particularly characteristic," the police clearly did not hesitate to arrest and deport individuals whose only offense was to have left their papers at home, persons traveling through Moscow or Leningrad, and peasants and seasonal workers, even if they had work certificates and other attestations. Anyone without papers in the "passportized zones" appeared ipso facto suspect, and even "socially harmful." Consider this memo addressed to the city police: "The police officer should always keep in mind that any individual without a passport, or any unregistered individual, is already a suspect individual who has either committed a crime and has escaped from prison, from a camp, or from deportation and is trying to cover his tracks, or is about to commit a crime."[43]

According to the administrative circulars in force, violators of the laws regulating residence in cities "subject to special rules" could be sentenced, depending on the specific case and the presumed degree of their "social dangerousness," to fines, immediate or deferred expulsion with a prohibition on residing in a certain number of cities, deportation with the status of special settler or labor colonist, or detention in a labor camp for a maximum term of three years. Special police commissions were authorized to hand down these sentences after an accelerated procedure in which the offender did not appear.[44] In reality, even this minimal procedure was far from always being respected, especially when the machinery spun out of control, while the number of cases to be dealt with was increasing. That was exactly what happened at the end of April 1933. It seems that the great majority of the individuals arrested and deported were rounded up on April 27, 28, and 29, at the very time that the police launched a vast operation intended to "cleanse" Moscow and Leningrad before the Labor Day festivities on May 1. During this period, being on the streets without your passport could have serious consequences. Witness the following cases, among a long list of similar examples:

V. Novolojilov, "Muscovite, stoker in the Kompressor factory, three-time award winner. Wife and child duly registered in Moscow. After work, he was preparing to go to the movies with his wife. While she was getting ready, he went out to buy cigarettes. Rounded up and deported."

G. Nazin, "Muscovite, chief assistant in the fire brigade at the Bolshoi Theater, member of the Kremlin fire brigade. Rounded up in the street. The Kremlin pass Nazin showed the police was not taken into consideration."

N. V. Voikin, "member of the Communist Youth since 1929, worker at the Krasnyi Tkatch (Red Weaver) Mill in Serpukhov. Member of the office of the Party cell in his workshop, candidate for the mill's plenary committee. Three-time award winner. Arrested in the street as he was going to a soccer match. Had left his passport at home."

Chmelev, "member of the Communist Youth since the beginning of 1933, worker in the Frounze Factory in Moscow, carpenter. Was supposed to receive his passport in two days. Had a receipt to this effect in proper form. Arrested in the street as he was returning home from work. The receipt was of no use."

N. V. Chudkov, "member of the Communist Youth, assistant director of the Nejiltrest Cooperative (Leninskii district, Moscow), has a brother who is a scholarship student at the Industrial Academy. Went to see the opera "The Queen of Spades" at the Bolshoi Theater. As he left the theater, he was arrested in Neglinnaia Street and deported to Nazino. Had left his passport at home."

Pavel Alexeievich Tkachev, "had just joined the Communist Youth in March 1933, card. no. 1387815, and had paid his dues until August, a fact certified on the card that he has managed to retain. Tkachev was a resident of the orphanage run by the Central Executive Committee in Moscow, and was living in Pushkino for the summer. Tkachev and another resident of the orphanage, Vassiliev, had been told to collect all the wind instruments left in the orphanage buildings in Moscow in order to prepare for the concert on May 1. The administration had given them all the necessary documents, certificates, and attestations. As he was getting off the suburban train, Tkachev was arrested and deported. His Communist Youth card and other documents were of no help."

Maslov, "Party member, worked in the Moscow gas plant. Had invited an engineer friend and his brother-in-law to his house for a drink. All three went out to buy snacks and were arrested by a police patrol at the food store. Had not taken their passports along. Were deported. The engineer and the brother-in-law died in Nazino. Maslov survived."[45]

Moscow residents legally residing in the capital and arrested in the street by random police patrols represent, however, only a minority of the cases of deportation judged abusive. The majority concern persons who were temporarily staying in the capital or passing through it, and who had usually been arrested in train stations, despite all the certificates and other attestations that had been given them by their government office, their company, or their kolkhoz. Among the cases considered "particularly representative" are the following:

Sergei Andreievich Voronine, "railway mechanic, employed in the 13th section of the Leningrad-Moscow railway, arrested in the Moscow train station as he was passing through the capital on his way back from his annual holiday and with his travel order properly certified."

Feodosii Mikhailovich Artiukh, "born 1912, kolkhozian in the Lenin Kolkhoz, in the town of Teplovka, Prilutskii district, Ukraine Soviet Socialist Republic. Sent by his kolkhoz, along with three other kolkhozians, to buy bread in Moscow All four were arrested as they got off the train. The three other kolkhozians, all from the same village—Mikhail Komskii, Ivan Volotskii, and Ivan Tikhenko—died on the island of Nazino. When they arrested the four kolkhozians, the transportation police refused to even glance at the kolkhoz's attestations certifying that F. M. Artiukh and his three companions were duly mandated."

Rakhametzianova, "12 years old, does not speak Russian. Was in transit in Moscow. Her mother left her alone in the station while she went to try to buy bread. The girl was arrested by the police as a young vagabond and deported alone to Narym."

Nikolay Iakovlevich Mosalikin, "candidate for membership in the Party since 1932, team leader in the kolkhoz of the village of Nevedomyi Kolodets, in the Belgorod region. Sent on a mission by his kolkhoz to buy bread in Moscow. Arrested as he got off the train. Had all his certificates in order. The police refused to look at them. Deported to Narym."

Galina Georguievna Gorbunova, "wife of the reserve commander of the cruiser *Aurora*, arrested while she was passing through a Moscow train station on her way home to Leningrad, and while she was pregnant. Had with her all her papers and her train ticket for Leningrad. Gave birth on the island of Nazino."[46]

The arrests, immediately followed by deportation, could strike—as a certain number of examples show—those whom Velichko described as "comrades socially close to the Soviet government." Nonetheless, among the persons arrested in and around the train stations, one category was clearly predominant: peasants fleeing famine who had reached the capital despite all the obstacles put in their way, ranging from the suspension of railway ticket sales to the deployment of special units of the OGPU's Transportation Department that were charged with tracking down "fugitives spreading rumors about alleged food supply problems." During these months of famine in the spring of 1933, peasants, whether they arrived alone or with their families, were systematically arrested, whether or not they had been officially sent by their kolkhozes, whether or not they had an employment contract, whether or not they were supervised by a recruiting agent for a company or a construction project. When they were, Velichko emphasized, it was not rare for the recruiting agent to be arrested and deported along with "his" men.[47]

According to the testimony collected, persons who were arrested spent very little time in police stations (twenty-four to forty-eight hours) before being put, without further ado, in the OGPU's convoys headed for Siberia. "Poezjaite, tam s vami razberutsja!" (Just leave, they'll clear up your case out there!) That was the standard reply given by police officials to protests by people who had been arrested, who were not even authorized to inform their families or friends, if they had any.[48] The police not only paid no attention to documents, attestations, certificates, or union or political party cards when they were presented, but in addition frequently confiscated them, no doubt so that they would not have give explanations regarding the identity of déclassé elements arrested and deported—the police forces' immediate goal being, as the Kovalev Commission noted, "to fill the convoys and to report results in numbers."[49] During the ten-day trip to Tomsk, deportees who had managed to hang onto their papers often lost them to the extortion of common criminals, who "used them to roll their cigarettes."[50] The forced cohabitation of delinquents and "or-

dinary citizens" gave rise to a violent situation in which
the most inveterate stole from the "novices" not only
their meager rations (300 grams of bread per day, and
nothing more) but also their clothes, their money, and
their papers. In the convoy that departed Moscow on
April 30, a band of delinquents led by a certain Mako-
veiev, nicknamed Kolka the Sailor, seems to have attacked in particular "individuals socially close to the government" who had been deported by chance. Kolka the
Sailor "beat these people with a big stick on which he
had carved with his knife: "Government Decree of August 7, 1932.""[51] Several dozen deportees were "savagely
beaten" by this band, whose members were finally arrested on the convoy's arrival in Novosibirsk.[52] In Cheli-
abinsk, and then in Omsk, the convoy took on several
hundred additional detainees, to whom were added, all
along the way, a certain number of individuals put on
the convoy by chance. According to the testimony collected by the Kovalev Commission, the guards of the
OGPU's Transportation department who were responsible for escorting the déclassé elements often resorted to
heavy-handed tactics. The commission of inquiry's report mentioned, "as examples of individuals rounded up
by chance along the way," the following cases:

"N. S. Skripov, was going to Ichim with his family, but
since access to this city had been closed because of an
epidemic, he found himself in Omsk. Arrested in the
market by guards who were escorting a column of detainees, and loaded on the convoy of deportees head-
ing for the transit camp in Tomsk. From there, sent to
Nazino."

"Egor Slesarenko, aged fifteen, apprentice railway worker in Omsk. Picked up by chance by the guards of the convoy when the latter stopped in the Omsk train station. Deported to Nazino."

"Nikolay Fedorovich Kurtiukov, sixteen, residing in Moscow. . . . Returning to Moscow after a visit to his stepfather, I. V. Berezin, a battalion commander stationed in Voeinnyi Poselok, near Vladivostok. Got off the passenger train in the Maslianinskaia station to look for boiling water to make tea. Arrested by the guard of the convoy of deportees coming from Moscow, which had stopped on another track. Put in the convoy by force, deported to Tomsk, then to Nazino."

"B. F. Oussenko, accountant, residing in Kursk. Had taken the train to go to the Golutvino station, but did not awaken in time. Seeing the convoy of deportees stopped in the station, he asked the guards to let him ride along to get to Golutvino. Having raised his voice [*sic*] he was immediately arrested, put on the convoy, and deported to the Narym region. B. F. Oussenko is a former Red Army volunteer and a reserve officer."[53]

When they arrived in the Tomsk transit camp on May 10, the déclassé elements from Moscow and Leningrad seemed from the outset, according to the testimony of Kuznetsov, the head of the camp, "particularly agitated." On the second night after the convoy's arrival, disturbances broke out in one of the wooden huts into which several hundred deportees had been crowded. The mounted police were called in. The situation was particularly confused, Kuznetsov acknowledged, "because the camp was plunged into the deepest darkness, since the Siblag had not had time to install electrical lighting." In the early hours of the morning, guards and representatives of the administration finally managed to gain entry into the hut. In fact, all the deportees were demanding was water. For two days, they had not received any water and all they had had to eat was a little bread and salt fish.[54] According to Sokolov, the Siblag's chief assistant, the disturbances were in fact caused by something far more serious: the guards had opened fire on deportees who were trying to escape from the hut; the day before, Kuznetsov had taken away seven "socially dangerous elements" and "ringleaders," pretended to execute them, and let it be known that any other troublemakers would meet the same fate.[55] The situation remained explosive.

With its 25,000 deportees—a third of whom were classified as "urban déclassé and socially dangerous elements"—the Tomsk transit camp seemed to both the city authorities and the leaders of the Siblag to be a real powder keg—especially since, according to the plan distributed to the camp authorities, some 350,000 deportees were supposed to pass through it in three months, with 4,000 being "dispatched" daily to the komandaturas in the Narym region. Since the degree of congestion in the camp was becoming catastrophic, getting rid of the most troubled contingents seemed the highest priority. It was in these circumstances that on May 14, 1933, several thousand "elements" were hastily put on barges headed for the Alexandro-Vakhovskaia komandatura.

CHAPTER 5

Nazino

On May 5, 1933, Tsepkov, the commander of the Alexandro-Vakhovskaia komandatura, received two telegrams. One was from the Siblag leadership, informing him that he must prepare himself "to receive, as soon as navigation conditions permit, 3,000 déclassé elements arriving from Tomsk." The second, which came from the Tomsk transit camp, confirmed this information, but gave a still higher figure, on the order of 5,000 to 6,000 "elements."[1]

"Taken completely by surprise," as he himself said, Tsepkov first called a meeting of the komandatura's few officials. Each one said that nothing was ready, since the deportees had not been expected to arrive before the end of June. Moreover, up to that point the Siblag had never said that it would be sending a massive number of deportees consisting exclusively of urban déclassé elements to the Alexandro-Vakhovskaia komandatura. Thus they had been expecting to have to "deal with the usual contingents of kulaks and a few urban elements." In addition, they had still received no word regarding the boats that had been promised by the Rechtrans for transporting the deportees up the Ob's tributaries to their settlement sites; the construction of a central bread bakery in the town of Alexandrovskoie was stalled; food stocks were at their lowest point, because the ice breakup on the river had just begun and for months no riverboats had been able to come up the Ob. Other stocks, particularly "manufactured goods," were virtually nonexistent: in all, there were only thirty pairs of men's trousers, six sheets of tinplate—enough to make two dozen pails—and a few hundred pairs of *lapti* (hemp boots).[2] Tsepkov immediately sent a telegram to the Siblag leadership, explaining that it would be several weeks before he would be able to "receive" the deportees. He was wasting his time. The same evening, Novosibirsk indicated that the dispatch of contingents was now the province of the authorities at the Tomsk transit camp, which was very congested, and that Tsepkov had to conform to Kuznetsov's dispatching plans.[3] The commander then asked the help of the Party's District Committee. Vlassov, the secretary of the Alexandrovskoie district, called an emergency meeting. There could be no question of contesting the Siblag's decision. "Since a Party member transmitted the Siblag's directive to us, the latter is Party directive, and thus as Communists we have to carry it out," Vlassov explained.[4]

There was a discussion regarding the place where the déclassé elements should be disembarked. This contingent was particularly troubling for local officials, who had little familiarity with "this kind of group." "It was the first time I had to deal with that kind of group," Tsepkov explained before the commission of inquiry. "I've always worked in the countryside. I got to know the kulak; I was perfectly acquainted with the muzhik. I admit that when I found out that I would have to deal with socially harmful elements coming from the cities, I panicked."[5] However, Tspekov added, he was not the only one. "Everyone agreed that we couldn't unload these elements in either Alexandrovskoie or near the village where the former kulaks and Ostyaks had already settled. If we did that, all Hell would break loose. It would be the end of collectivization, cooperatives, and the Ostyaks. They would steal everything, pillage everything, and massacre the local people."[6]

Hence it was decided, according to Tsepkov, to unload the déclassé elements on an island in the middle of the Ob, located opposite the village of Nazino, seventy kilometers upstream from Alexandrovskoie. From there, they would be taken by boat, in scattered groups, to their "final place of settlement," far from any inhabited area, along the Nazina River, one of the Ob's numerous tributaries. Tsepkov's version was contested by Vlassov, who stated before the commission of inquiry that after an animated discussion the Party District Committee finally decided to unload the deportees near the village of Proletarka. Thus it was Tsepkov himself who chose, at the last moment and despite the "Party's directives," to disembark the deportees on the island of Nazino.[7]

The questions of how to transport and supply the deportees were also discussed at this meeting. Since the komandatura lacked everything, it was decided to "ask all the kolkhozes, rural soviets, and other economic organizations in the district to provide, within two weeks, hatchets, saws, shovels, and other tools needed to enable the new contingents to build shelters, and to mobilize all available motorboats and rowboats to carry the deportees from the point where they were taken off the larger riverboats to their settlement sites." The Executive Committee of the soviets was asked to "make available to Commander Tsepkov the food stocks in cooperative storehouses, on the express condition that he will promptly replenish the quantities allocated." Finally, "in order to prevent mass escapes and the inevitable increase in thefts that usually follows the unloading of such a large number of déclassés," the local authorities were called upon to "strengthen the population's vigilance and capacity for self-defense, to organize night patrols, and to do everything possible to arrest fugitives."[8] These fighting words remained largely just that—words. The kolkhozes were struggling along with barely enough means of production to survive, and they lacked food supplies: for the past two years, food shortages had been endemic everywhere in the Narym region.

In the meantime, 900 kilometers away, the authorities in the Tomsk transit camp were hastily preparing to send on the déclassé elements from Moscow and Leningrad. Before May 15, 16,000 deportees coming from Ukraine and the North Caucasus were expected in addition to the approximately 25,000 deportees already in the camp. "I had to receive two, sometimes three convoys a day, and to send out the same number," Kuznetsov, the head of the camp, told the commission of inquiry. "That's why I was unable to supervise in detail the sending out of the four barges full of deportees on May 14."[9] All the camp's officials were overworked; a certain Kolubaiev, who had been "recommended by the Party Committee of Tomsk, but had no experience working with special settlers," was asked to supervise the operations of loading and

convoying some 5,000 "elements" as far as the Alexandro-Vakhovskaia komandatura.

The Rechtrans made available to the camp four barges
that were normally used for transporting wood and were
completely unsuited for conveying thousands of persons. The sole adaptation made for the purpose was a
hastily constructed barrier to separate the men from the
women. Since the contingent was considered "particularly dangerous and likely to try to escape,"[10] Kolubaiev
was ordered not to stop for any reason during the five-
or six-day trip up the river to the debarkation point. All
the deportees were crowded below decks, "with no opportunity to go on deck, so that on arrival many of the
people, completely overwhelmed by the pure air of the
taiga, fainted, whereas hundreds of others who were unable to move had to be pulled out onto the riverbank."[11]
To feed the deportees en route, Tsepkov gave them the
"prescribed ration"—five days' worth of bread, at a rate
of 200 grams per person, plus—he claimed—enough
flour, salt, sugar, and dried fish for a month.[12]

In reality, as came out in the contradictory testimony
collected by the commission of inquiry, the provisions
taken on board in addition to the "prescribed ration of
bread" consisted in no more than a few sacks of semolina, sugar, and salt, along with twenty tons of flour, or
four kilos per person, enough to last ten days—but only
if the flour was made into bread. However, the barges
being overloaded, nothing else was taken along—no
cooking utensils, dishes, bowls, or tools that might have
enabled the deportees to make food for themselves or
set up rudimentary shelters.

Questioned regarding this "thoughtless dispatch of thin, ragged, poorly clothed, nearly shoeless individuals, with not even a bowl to eat in, not even a cup or spoon," Kuznetsov retorted:

> I was convinced that the commanders to whom we were sending this contingent were properly prepared to receive it, since they had received all the necessary instructions during the meeting that had been held in March . . . moreover, had I gone beyond the norm, I would certainly have been accused of sabotage or, more likely, of yielding to the dizziness of success[13] . . . finally, I had been told by the leadership that if the deportees were not correctly clothed, if they had not brought along with them the fifty to one hundred kilos to which they had a right under the regulations, it was not up to the Siblag to provide them with clothing and provisions.[14]

Again, "in accord with the hygienic norms relating to the conveying of special settlers," a physician and two health officers, equipped with five small rural pharmaceutical kits, were assigned to the convoy.

A final, particularly delicate point remained to be dealt with: there was a desperate lack of guards to escort these thousands of déclassé elements. For the usual convoys of kulaks deported along with their families, the prescribed "norm" was one guard for every hundred families. For the urban déclassés, the norm was one guard for every hundred individuals. Finding some fifty guards to escort the May 14 convoy proved a difficult task, and the authorities ended up recruiting poor, unemployed wretches who had been wandering the streets of Tomsk. As Tsepkov said in his deposition,

> these people, who had neither shoes nor uniforms, were in no way distinguished from the déclassé elements they were supposed to monitor. They had neither authority nor discipline. If they gave an order, no one listened to them. "Look at yourself, you're no different from me," these elements replied. When I gave them [the guards] an order, they ignored me. We had hardly arrived in Nazino before most of them told me that they wanted to go back to Tomsk, because they had been tricked. When they were recruited, they had been promised that the komandatura would take care of them, give them a uniform, shoes, and lodging in Alexandrovskoie. However, all they got was an old rifle, and then they were sent into the taiga to have the people "graze," as they called it.[15]

Under such conditions, is it surprising that most of these guards stole from the deportees and subjected them to every conceivable or imaginable kind of extortion? In addition to the fifty or so guards, the Siblag sent two newly recruited commanders to the special villages, under orders to help Kolubaiev, the head of the convoy, and to back up the little team at the Alexandro-Vakhovskaia komandatura.

At five p.m. on May 15, Tsepkov received a telegram from Kuznetsov informing him that the day before he had sent him two convoys of four barges with 4,900 déclassés on board. These convoys arrived at the Verkhne-

Vartovsk pier on May 18. There, Kuznetsov was supposed to handle the operations and unload the deportees "at the planned settlement sites." Did the head of the Tomsk camp know exactly where the deportees were going to be set ashore, and under what conditions? In his deposition before the commission, he asserted that he did not—Tsepkov had telegraphed him to say that the place of debarkation would be "between the villages of Nazino and Proletarka," without specifying the precise site. According to Kuznetsov, Tsepkov had not properly informed him of his state of complete unpreparedness. Tsepkov had transmitted his grievances directly to his superiors in Novosibirsk, and they had not forwarded them. All in all, a fairly common situation. Despite all the "plans," the settlement of the deportees had always been carried out, in the end, *na khodu*, "on the spur of the moment," without preparation.[16]

Travelling upstream against the current on the only usable motorboat the komandatura had at that time, and accompanied by two assistants and three guards, it took Tsepkov three days to cover the 150 kilometers separating Alexandrovskoie from Verkne-Vartovsk. When he arrived there, he took over the direction of the operations and had the convoys land several dozen kilometers downstream, on a deserted island in the middle of the Ob. This island was three kilometers long and some 500 to 600 meters wide, and was situated across the river from the little village of Nazino, where a few special settler families and a few dozen Ostyak families lived. Like most of the islands in the Ob, which was more than two kilometers wide at this point, it was flooded at times of high water and offered only an inhospitable expanse of swamps and poplar groves.

We have several accounts, which corroborate each other to a remarkable extent, regarding the debarkation of some 5,000 déclassé elements on the island of Nazino on the afternoon of May 18, 1933.[17] These accounts enable us to reconstruct the scene.

Until nightfall, Tsepkov; his assistant in charge of accounting, Kiselev; and Kolubaiev, the head of the convoy, kept busy for hours trying to count the deportees and perform a roll call. An impossible task: the lists, written in pencil on wrapping paper, were for the most part illegible; in addition, the number of individuals they mentioned—5,318—differed both from the number of "passengers" registered on departure that Kuznetsov had communicated—4,900—and from the number—5,000—telegraphed to Tsepkov by the Siblag's Department of Special Settlements. As it was getting dark and the captain of the river convoys was threatening to "demand a supplementary payment for immobilizing his boats" if he was late in leaving for Tomsk, Tsepkov decided not to do an individual roll call, and to limit himself to counting the persons unloaded. The women were made to disembark first—there were 322 of them—and then the men, who numbered 4,556. Twenty-seven bodies of deportees who had died during the transfer from Tomsk were also unloaded.[18]

As all the witnesses acknowledged, a very large number of deportees—at least a third—were so emaciated and weak that they were no longer able to stand. Tsepkov ordered several dozen of the more able-bodied deportees to get the weaker ones out of the hold. In his deposition, the commander did not conceal his stupefaction on first seeing this "contingent":

> I'd never lived in the city; I had no idea what these criminal and urban déclassé elements were like. I'd imagined they would be very different from these injured and ill people, these poor wretches with deathly pale faces, most of them in rags, a few dressed in city clothes, with shoes and a coat, but all of them without even a bag, even the good old big canvas bag into which a peasant always succeeds in slipping some tool, a kettle, a knife, a cup, a piece of lard. All these people got off the boat—if they could still stand up— with nothing, without any provisions at all, empty-handed.[19]

Once the deportees had been set down on the island, Tsepkov ordered the twenty tons of flour unloaded. A fight broke out while the sacks of flour were being unloaded, and the guards opened fire, wounding several persons. After this incident, Tsepkov ordered the convoy to cast off and unload the stocks on the other side of the river, in Nazino, where they would be protected from any "attack." But not from the damp and the cold: in fact, because there were not enough sacks—a product always in short supply—a large portion of the flour loaded on the barges had been directly poured into sandbags that were deposited, not without difficulty, directly on the earth. The local inhabitants were stupefied by this "mountain of abundance," which was soon covered with snow, for a few hours after the boats were unloaded, a snowstorm began. This seriously aggravated the situation of the thousands of starving and chilled deportees, who began to light wood fires in the hope of warming themselves.

The next morning, on an island covered by a thin blanket of spring snow and the thick smoke from dozens of wood fires burning in the ambient dampness, Tsepkov, accompanied by his assistants, the three health officers, and the two new commanders who had arrived from Tomsk, tried to organize an initial distribution of flour, at the rate of one pound per person, no other foodstuff being available. Most of the deportees having no cup, tumbler, or any other container into which the precious ration could be put, "the luckiest held out their fur hats, and others their shoes or coattails, while the most deprived had nothing but their two hands to receive the prescribed measure."[20] After two hours, the distribution that the officials had tried to organize— despite the approximately 5,000 mouths to be fed—by handing out the provisions to individuals, "one by one, according to their place in line," degenerated into a disorderly scramble. Dozens—perhaps hundreds (on this point, the testimony differed)—of deportees were trampled. Once again, the guards, overwhelmed, opened fire, wounding several persons. Tsepkov had the distribution halted and announced new rules, which were to prove catastrophic for a number of the deportees, especially the weakest and least able to fight for survival. The distribution would henceforth be made by "brigadiers" who would receive daily from the administration a ration of seventy-five kilos for one hundred and fifty persons. This system led to the greatest abuses, since a minority of criminals, more ruthless than the others, immediately monopolized the positions of "brigadiers" and the operations of distribution.[21]

After the morning's incidents, Tsepkov tried to put together two teams of deportees who knew how to construct primitive clay ovens for baking bread like the ones peasants built in the countryside. About thirty volunteers were taken, under close escort, to Nazino. However, this experiment did not succeed. Because the earth was frozen below the surface, the volunteers were not able to dig deep enough; the small amount of clay they found was of poor quality; and especially, according to Tsepkov, "the déclassé elements all claimed to know all sorts of trades, but when they were put to work, they didn't know how to do anything, and especially not how to build bread ovens."[22]

On the island, the dead were piling up. In the mission report Kolubaiev, the head of the convoy, submitted on his return to Tomsk he wrote:

At two p.m. on May 20, I went to the island of Nazino with Commander Tsepkov. There was a terrible scramble, people crowding and fighting around the bags of flour, dead bodies everywhere, a hundred or more, and lots of people crawling about and crying "Give us bread. Boss, it's been two days since we've been given anything to eat—they're trying to make us die of hunger and the cold." They told us that people had begun eating the dead bodies, that they were cooking human flesh. The scene on the island was DREADFUL, APPALLING. When we got back to the village of Nazino, we gathered together all the assistant commanders and health personnel—barely a dozen persons in all. It was decided (1) to set up a few tents to shelter the most sick; (2) to mobilize the local population to construct ovens; (3) to requisition all the ovens of the inhabitants of the village of Nazino (ten to twelve homes). Having thus completed my mission, I left for Tomsk with the convoy at three a.m. on May 21.[23]

Confronted by growing chaos, Tsepkov decided to go to see what he could find in the way of food supplies and equipment in Alexandrovskoie, delegating his powers to Chikhalev and Suleimainov, the two commanders who had come from Tomsk.

Over the next few days, the situation on the island grew steadily worse. Apart from a few dozen fortunate invalids who had been put into the four tents set up by the health officers and to whom bread and semolina soup were distributed, the immense majority of the deportees had to get along on a ration of one pound of flour a day mixed with a little river water—which immediately caused serious intestinal disturbances. The ration was, moreover, purely theoretical, since many deportees received nothing at all after the distribution was taken over by the gangsters and the guards—the latter "differing from the former only because they carried firearms."[24] To get their ration, as small as it might be, deportees who still had a few warm clothes, an overcoat, or a pair of shoes had to give them up in exchange for a piece of bread or a pound of flour. According to testimony collected by Velichko, in the "primitive socialist economy" that rapidly established itself on the island, a pair of shoes was worth three one-kilo loaves of bread or five salt fish, and an overcoat could be exchanged for a two-kilo loaf of bread, a package of tobacco, or two gold dental crowns.[25]

In his account, already quoted, Ivan Ionovich Ouvarov refers to other "equivalencies" current on Nazino: one gold crown for a box of matches or a newspaper (used mainly for rolling cigarettes).[26] The practice of extracting gold crowns from the jawbones of cadavers is mentioned as early as May 23 in the first report submitted by the physician and the two health officers in charge of the sanitary situation on the island.[27] As more and more deportees died, this practice turned into a regular business that left a lasting impression on people's minds because it marked a major transgression against the respect due to the dead. These gold crowns immediately found buyers among the traffickers and gold traders of the Russian "Far East"; they were resold, usually illicitly, to the cooperatives of the Torgsin network in exchange for products that were in short supply and were particularly prized.[28]

The guards' activities were not limited, alas, to experimenting with the implementation of a "primitive socialist economy." Using and abusing their power, the armed guards instituted a reign of arbitrariness and terror, and did not hesitate to summarily execute deportees who "cheated" during the distribution of food,'[29] or to kill in order to steal an overcoat or a pair of shoes. In this respect, the wealthiest deportees from Moscow and Leningrad who had been arrested and deported as a result of some unfortunate chance seem to have also been the most vulnerable—although the jackets, overcoats, or shoes they wore could serve as money allowing them to obtain a bit of food, this coveted merchandise could also get its owner attacked and killed, as is shown by numerous examples cited by the commission of inquiry.

If the guards committed the most widespread and most murderous atrocities, Chikhalev, Suleimanov, and a half-dozen other commanders in neighboring special villages who were called upon to help committed their share as well. The commission of inquiry's report cited some of the atrocities committed by the supervisory staff:

> Vlassenko, commander of the village of Nazino: "blows and injuries systematically inflicted on special settlers; systematic nondistribution of provisions; deportees who did not know how to swim were thrown overboard and drowned."

> Tsarapkin, commander of the village of Proletarka, "amused himself by having special settlers row the boats. Those who rowed badly were thrown in the water. Several deportees drowned in this way."

> Khokhlov, manager of the cooperative storehouse in Nazino, "systematically beat special settlers with a stick, extorted clothing from them by promising them better rations, forced special settlers to leap into the freezing water of the river to fetch the water birds he had shot."

> Chikhalev, commander of the island of Nazino, "set an example by systematically beating with a stick special settlers who fell into his hands and indulging in speculation and trafficking in clothing stolen from

special settlers and in gold crowns taken from the mouths of the dead."

Suleimanov, commander of the island of Nazino, "beat special settlers with a stick, used them as oarsmen when he went fishing. Behaved inappropriately with regard to individuals who were starving."[30]

In his letter to Stalin, Velichko provides some illuminating details concerning the "inappropriate behavior" on Commander Sulemanov's part that was singled out for criticism by the commission of inquiry: "In front of starving deportees awaiting their meager ration of flour, he ostentatiously ate huge quantities of sugar, to the point that, as he himself said, he completely lost his taste for it."[31]

This kind of "abuse" on the part of the supervisory staff, which was qualified by the commission of inquiry as "seigneurial behavior," was in reality—as is shown by the numerous administrative reports concerning everyday life in the "special villages"—very widespread among the "little bosses" of the komandaturas, and even among the local Communist officials, who constituted a new stratum of "sovereign serfs"[32] who were prompt to parody the stereotypical behavior that the state that arose out of the October Revolution attributed to the overthrown former masters.

However, the most serious facts that came to light concerned the murder of deportees, who were "shot as in hunting"—a practice that was, as we have seen, far from exceptional in the komandaturas of the Narym region. In their defense, the guards and commanders implicated by the commission of inquiry referred to the orders Tsepkov had given to immediately fire on anyone trying to escape. And in fact it seems that many deportees did try to flee on small, primitive rafts. "At first," one official explained,

> we didn't think anyone could escape from the island of Nazino; the current was very strong, the water was freezing cold, and the river was several kilometers wide. Without tools, they couldn't build a boat. But a certain number of criminal and déclassé elements showed great ingenuity: by tying large, dry branches together, they were able to make a sort of primitive raft that could carry three or four people. Then they let the current carry them along. A persistent rumor was going around to the effect that about sixty kilometers downstream there was a railway line that would enable them to get back to Novosibirsk. . . . Naturally, the fugitives had very little chance of surviving. Most of them drowned or died of hunger. We found, for dozens of kilometers downstream, hundreds of bodies that had washed up on the banks of the Ob.[33]

For the chekist officials, the fugitive "criminal and déclassé elements" were dangerous individuals who had to be eliminated for at least two reasons: they were likely to join (as other fugitives had already done) the "criminal bands of bandits" still active in the Narym region, and in addition, some of them were "particularly degenerate individuals"—in short, cannibals.

"Strange things are happening in Russia. Famine, cannibalism. . . . People arriving from the provinces tell odd stories," Nina Lugovskaia, a young student in Moscow who came from a well-off family of the city's intelligentsia, wrote in her diary.[34] At the same time, the OGPU's postal censors were confiscating thousands of letters from Ukrainian peasants describing in detail the effects of the famine and the spread of anthropophagy in the countryside.[35] A few months earlier, in Kemorovo, a major mining center in the Kuzbass some 200 kilometers south of Tomsk, hundreds of Kazakhs fleeing famine had been lynched because rumors accused them of kidnapping Russian children in order to eat them.[36] In 1933, the USSR was buzzing with rumors of cannibalism. In the areas where the famines were most severe, these rumors were sometimes not unfounded. And even when they were unfounded, they were nonetheless, to use Marc Bloch's fine formulation, "the mirror in which the collective consciousness looks at its own face"[37]—despite the prohibition on looking at it, one is tempted to add in the specific case of the USSR in the early 1930s. In fact, perhaps even more than famine, which was unthinkable in the country of socialism, anthropophagy remained the taboo subject par excellence—the confidential instructions given by the OGPU's Department of Information, which was asked to look into the reactions of the population "with respect to rumors about the existence of problems with food supplies," are very explicit on this point[38]—but it was nonetheless on everyone's mind.

On the island of Nazino, the first rumors about "bodies cut up and human flesh cooked and eaten"[39] began to appear the day after the deportees were unloaded there. Three days later, on May 23, the three health officers on the island wrote the first report on the situation on Nazino, which they submitted to the Siblag's Department of Special Settlements. After describing the conditions under which the deportees had been "received" on the island, they alerted their superiors to the looming threat of a typhus epidemic. Five suspected cases had already been seen. But the bulk of the report deals with the rapidly rising mortality rate due to dysentery resulting from eating flour mixed with river water and to the generally weakened condition connected with weeks of insufficient nutrition—the deportees had not had any hot food since being arrested in Moscow or Leningrad. On May 21 alone, the three health officers counted seventy additional dead bodies.[40] "In five cases," they emphasized,

> the liver, the heart, the lungs, and fleshy parts of the bodies (breasts, calves) had been cut off. On one of the bodies, the head had been torn off, along with the male genital organs and part of the skin. These mutilations constitute strong evidence of cannibalistic acts; in addition, they suggest the existence of serious psychopathologies. On the same day, May 21, the deportees themselves brought us three individuals who had been caught with blood on their hands and holding human livers. Our examination of these three individuals did not reveal any extreme emaciation, but rather external signs of degeneracy. These individuals were immediately turned over to the head of the guard.[41]

In the course of the following weeks, the same health officers on the island submitted three additional reports describing analogous cases—in all "several dozen bodies found with the liver, heart, and lungs cut out."[42] According to the doctors, the guards and commanders had

hardly reacted—at least during the first days afterward—or taken any steps to isolate the individuals
caught in possession of human flesh or in the act of
eating it. Most of these individuals were released, since
"it had not been established that they had killed the person whose body parts they had eaten," and since "the
Soviet penal code does not prescribe a penalty for necrophagy."[43]

However, the first case in which murder followed by
acts of cannibalism was proven was recorded only on
May 29. The three guilty persons—young habitual criminals ranging in age from twenty to twenty-five—were
arrested and taken to the prison in Alexandrovskoie.
Three other cannibals were arrested on May 31. They
admitted having killed a young man and then eaten his
liver and kidneys. Visibly upset by this event, local officials tried at first to minimize and trivialize it. In his report to the Regional Committee of the Party in Narym,
Vlassov, the Party's district secretary, who had arrived
on the site May 31, devoted barely three lines to the
subject: "About a dozen cases of cannibalism have been
noted. According to the physicians, the individuals who
committed these acts of cannibalism were not completed
emaciated and starving. They indulged in cannibalism by
habit, because they had been cannibals for a long
time."[44] "Cannibalism by habit"—this astonishing explanation is also found in the deposition of Semernev, another local official questioned by the commission of inquiry.[45] But it is found as well in the juicy neologism
coined by the health officer Khatskelevich, an official at
the Alexandro-Vakhovskaia komandatura, who explained these acts of cannibalism as resulting from "ot-

tanism"[46]—a term borrowed, as such and without any reservations, by Ivan Dolguikh, the head of the Special Settlements Department, in the report he wrote on the Nazino affair for submission to Alexandr Gorchkov, the head of the Siblag.[47]

In referring to "cannibalism by habit" the officials of the Gulag were certainly thinking of a practice that was widespread in the particularly ruthless world of hardened criminals, that of "bleeding the cow." In the argot of the underworld, Jacques Rossi explains in his *Manuel du Goulag*,

> the "cow" is a novice whom the ex-convicts ask to join them in attempting to escape. In general, the novice is flattered to find himself associating with famous criminals. However, he does not know that if they run short of food, he will be killed, and his kidneys and his blood eaten (usually raw, the fugitives not daring to light a fire for fear of being spotted). In the camps and prisons, cow eaters are called cannibals. Cannibalism is not peculiar to the Soviet period. Under the Czars, a certain V. Vassiliev escaped from jail along with another prisoner. Before being caught, he had eaten his companion's flesh. But it was not until the establishment of the Soviet system that the phenomenon, which had become fairly frequent, gave rise to a series of specific slang terms (the cow; synonyms: the baggage, the ram, the lamb).[48]

Several of the guards indicted by the commission of inquiry for having "killed with rifles, as if they were hunting" deportees who were trying to escape on improvised rafts argued in their own defense that a number of these deportees who had "left in groups of three or four were certainly cannibals, taking along their cow." Thus we see emerging, in the minds of the officials and low-level staff, a first "explanation" of the acts of cannibalism committed on Nazino.

The testimonies collected in the late 1980s in Nazino and neighboring villages include other particularly striking images that suggest acts different from those associated with the practice—fairly well-attested in the criminal underworld—of "bleeding the cow." Thus four remarkably concordant testimonies[49] mention several cases of women being savagely attacked by "cannibals" who cut off their breasts or calves. Some of them survived, whereas others died of their wounds, and still others "went mad"[50] after these particularly traumatic attacks. Two of the testimonies mention in particular the case of "the wife of a Communist leader" who had been rounded up by chance in Moscow, deported to Tomsk, and then to Nazino, and whom "criminal elements" tortured by cutting off her breasts.[51] It was following this precise case that a "commission of leaders" is supposed to have finally been sent to Nazino to look into the cases of cannibalism. It has not proven possible to determine the identity of this "wife of a Communist leader" whose memory remained so vivid in the memories of the local residents. On the other hand, we do have a record of the meeting held on June 21 by a commission headed by Ivan Dolguikh and composed of Siblag officials that arrived on site more than a month after the déclassé and criminal elements were set down on the island of Nazino. In the passage of this commission's report relating to cannibalism, we find no explicit reference to the case of the "wife of a Communist leader." On the contrary, the Siblag officials sought to minimize the phenomenon of cannibalism while at the same time giving it a "political bent":

> Note that the rumors regarding cases of cannibalism systematically spread by the déclassés themselves are without foundation. These rumors obviously have political implications, as is shown by certain particular circumstances that are supposed to emphasize this aspect. Commander Tsepkov did not show Bolshevist vigilance in this regard. He did not locate the source of these rumors, did not expose the instigators, even though the latter were trying to turn the minds of the déclassé elements in a clearly anti-Soviet direction.[52]

In the "strictly confidential" report, already cited, that Ivan Dolguikh submitted to the leadership of the Siblag, the head of the Special Settlements Department developed a very political interpretation of the phenomenon of cannibalism.[53] He tried to demonstrate that "hunger cannot be the origin of these acts, given that most of the cases of cannibalism occurred at a time when the problem of provisions was being resolved. None of the cannibals caught showed signs of pronounced emaciation. Several of them admitted that in the past they had already eaten human flesh." However, Dolguikh did not accept "ottanism"—the neologism adopted by the head of the Siblag—as the main explanation of the cannibalism, "even if," he added, "a certain number of Party officials have lined up behind that argument." According to Dolguikh, the acts of cannibalism, which were often accompanied by "sadism," resulted in reality from a "peculiar combination of individual degeneracy and very well-defined political intentions." Among the latter was an attitude of defiance with regard to the Soviet regime, a defiance that a "criminal element," speaking to the head of the Siblag's Special Settlements Department, had put this way: "You're starving the people. Well, we're eating each other!"[54]

Cannibalism as a defiant response to the extreme violence practiced by a state that was starving people obviously constituted, in the eyes of the chekist officials, an unacceptably seditious notion. "I ordered the immediate arrest of this individual for counterrevolutionary propaganda," Dolguikh reported. During his brief stay in Nazino, he caused to be arrested about fifteen "ringleaders" who were making "counterrevolutionary statements and smugly spreading allegations regarding cannibalism and a famine allegedly organized by the Soviet state." According to Dolguikh, these rumors were relayed by a certain number of political exiles who had "come specially to the village of Nazino in order to establish contacts with the déclassé elements." All this, he concluded, "clearly demonstrates a political manipulation directed by outside elements."[55]

Precisely how widespread was cannibalism in Nazino? Even if it left an indelible impression—to which the well-attested nickname "Cannibal Island" bears witness—the number of proven cases of cannibalism and necrophagy was not more than a few dozen. About fifty persons suspected of having eaten human flesh were arrested, but many of them were quickly released. Given the very fragmentary evidence we have regarding the identity of these individuals, it would be risky to draw any conclusions about the "typical profile" of the "Nazino cannibal." Here we will limit ourselves to emphasizing that all the anthropophagi were men, most of whom were young, had been born in the countryside, had already been found guilty of crimes at least once, and had already done time in a camp or in prison.[56] Eleven cannibals were sentenced to death by a special OGPU panel specially set up in July 1933 for the purpose of "liquidating criminal activity in the Narym region."[57] These sentences were handed down after the OGPU's plenipotentiary representative personally intervened to overturn the decision made by the Narym region's prosecutor not to prosecute the individuals accused of necrophagy, on the ground that "eating human flesh is not subject to penalty in the Soviet penal code and the material conditions into which the labor colonists deported to the island of Nazino had been put were particularly difficult."[58] According to Ivan Ouvarov's testimony, the people who were eating human flesh were well aware that they could do so with impunity so long as it had not been proven that they had previously murdered the victim. As for spending a few months in prison while awaiting the investigation of his case, that meant, according to one of the cannibals arrested, "at least a guaranteed roof over [my] head and a bowl of hot *balanda* (a broth served in prisons and camps) instead of freezing to death and having to eat flour mixed with river water."[59]

The dramatic situation on the island of Nazino was still further aggravated on May 27, with the arrival of a new convoy of déclassé elements sent out from the transit camp a week earlier, even before Kolubaiev, the official in charge of the first two convoys, had returned to Tomsk. Obviously, the camp's authorities had not been informed of what was happening 900 kilometers downstream, and had continued to "decongest" the camp, at the rate of 3,000 to 4,000 individuals a day sent to the various komandaturas in the Narym region. On the evening of May 27, about 1,200 déclassé elements were crowded into the hold of a barge and sent over to the island of Nazino under approximately the same conditions as the 5,000 or so who had been sent earlier. According to the doctors on site, this second group was in an even more "degraded" state of health than the first one, a certain number of them suffering from typhus. It was decided to quarantine the sick on a part of the island, but everything was lacking: there were only six tents, and no medicines or even containers for boiling water in order to disinfect the clothing of the contaminated individuals. "In any case," the physicians wrote in their report, "the deportees' rags would not have survived any washing, and we would have found ourselves with totally naked individuals, while every night the temperature drops below freezing."[60] Like the contingents unloaded on May 18, the new arrivals received nothing to eat but a little flour, bread being reserved for the sickest among them.

Accompanied by Vlassov, the secretary of the Communist Party organization in the Alexandrovskoie district, Commander Tsepkov returned to Nazino on May 31, after more than a week's absence. In the interim, an emergency meeting of the Office of the District Committee of the Party had been called in the komandatura's

administrative center to decide what to do about the déclassé elements who had been unloaded on the island
of Nazino. After listening to Tsepkov's report, the Party
officials ordered the commander to transfer, within one
week (that is, before June 5), all the deportees to "appropriate places designated by the settlement plan"; to
mobilize the whole of the local population "for baking
bread and feeding the déclassé elements"; to requisition
among the local economic organizations "all the tools,
construction materials, and instruments necessary for
building shelters, the cooking utensils required for preparing hot meals, and all available boats." The resolution
adopted at the end of this meeting severely criticized
Commander Tsepkov, who was accused of "incompe-
tence" and "violating the Party's resolutions concerning
the reception of special settlers."[61] Shortly after he arrived in Nazino, Vlassov sent a long report to the Party
secretary for the Narym region, Levits, to inform him
about the situation.[62] At that time (early June), Tsepkov
had still not dared inform his superiors—that is, the
leaders of the Siblag, and in particular Ivan Dolguikh,
the head of the Department of Special Settlements—of
what had happened. It was through "Party channels"
that Robert Eikhe, the "boss" of Western Siberia,
learned, around June 10, about "the Nazino affair."

The report Vlassov sent his superiors in the first days of
June provides numerous details regarding the situation
on the island at that time, that is, about two weeks after
the arrival of the first convoys. At that date, when the
temperature was hovering around freezing, no hot
meals had yet been distributed to the deportees, for lack

not only of provisions, but also of pots and utensils that could be used to cook food. After ovens in the few surrounding villages had been requisitioned, a few tons of bread had been allocated to the deportees, a ridiculously small quantity to feed so many mouths. For weeks, the vast majority of the deportees had to survive on a daily ration of flour. Tsepkov and Vlassov had managed to bring back from Alexandrovskoie a few hundred tools (axes, shovels, saws), four hundred pairs of *lapti*, and several bundles of cloth. Except for the *lapti*, these supplies were in quantities very insufficient to provide shoes for thousands of barefoot deportees, the few bits of cloth requisitioned in the nearly empty depots of the few cooperative storehouses in this part of the Soviet world being of little use ("without a sewing machine," Tsepkov admitted before the commission of inquiry, "we couldn't do much with the cloth"). As for the axes, which were indispensable for cutting wood and building shelters, was it reasonable to put them into the hands of "socially dangerous elements" who were cannibals to boot? It was finally decided not to distribute these tools to the deportees when they were transferred from the island of Nazino to their "final settlement sites." For this transfer, Tsepkov and Vlassov had succeeded in mobilizing about twenty more or less usable boats, each of which could carry a few dozen persons. It was on this fleet that the deportees were taken, starting in early July, to their "final settlement sites." Five such sites up the Nazina River were chosen "on the recommendation of Suleimanov, who was well acquainted with the taiga and remembered places where there were a few hunters' huts and

where the fishing was good."[63] These places were between 60 and 120 kilometers from the island of Nazino,
a distance that it took the boats several days to travel,
going upstream against the current. Within two weeks,
the island was almost completely emptied. On June 12,
there remained on Nazino only 157 deportees who
could not be moved.[64]

During the transfer, several hundred detainees who
were already very weak died.[65] These deaths were in addition to some 1,500 to 2,000 deaths that had occurred
since the disembarkation on the island and in addition
to the hundreds of escapees who had disappeared.[66] According to the testimony of Ivan Ouvarov, the komandatura's assistant head accountant, 2,856 deportees were
sent by boat from the island to points upstream on the
Nazina River.[67] At the end of June, a count was made of
the deportees "present" in the various "settlement sites";
this count confirmed that about half of the approximately 6,000 persons set ashore on Nazino five or six
weeks earlier had disappeared.[68] When they arrived at
their "final settlement sites," the survivors found themselves in a situation almost identical with the one they
had known on the island, the only difference being that
they were more left to their own devices, the few guards
having returned to Nazino to get another group of deportees, leaving behind "a few provisions and tools to
construct shelters." It was during this stage in their long
journey that a large number of the deportees tried to
escape on improvised rafts. Most of the fugitives per-
ished when their rafts sank, the guards shot them, or
they got lost in the immensity of the Siberian taiga.

In the meantime, word of what had happened in Nazino had reached the region's highest political authorities. On June 12, Robert Eikhe demanded an explanation from the OGPU's plenipotentiary representative for Western Siberia, Alexeiev, and from the head of the Siblag, Gorchkov. While minimizing the "incident" ("We asked the Alexandro-Vakhovskaia komandatura to explain the cases of negligence observed when a group of déclassé elements was received," the two officials of the OGPU and the Siblag told Eikhe in a telegram),[69] Alexeiev and Gorchkov ordered Ivan Dolguikh, who was then making an inspection tour in the komandaturas around Tomsk, to go to Nazino to assess the situation.

Before the commission of inquiry, the head of the Siblag's Department of Special Settlements recounted in detail his "expedition to these remote places":[70]

The situation was critical everywhere. I had to go repeatedly to both Parabel and Kargasok, where typhus was ranging among the deportees, and to the Galkinskaia komandatura, where a situation was emerging that was, if not analogous to that in the Alexandro-Vakhovskaia komandatura, at least approaching it. The question of provisions was critical there because the boats belonging to the Gospar [the state river transportation company], an organization with which the Siblag had signed a contract to manage these matters, were immobilized. The Gospar had just received a shipment of German motors, but it did not have the refined oil necessary to run them. After a short stop in Parabel, where out of the 2,800 deportees who had just been disembarked there were 230 sick with typhus, I went directly to Alexandrovskoie, along with several collaborators, about twenty experienced armed guards and all the backup personnel I could find.[71]

Since the Siblag had made no means of transportation available to them, Dolguikh and his team finally reached Alexandrovskoie after six days' voyage on board the *Karl Marx*, the only boat making regular runs, two or three times during the navigable season, between Tomsk and Alexandrovskoie.

On June 21, the "inspection team," which had been joined by Commander Tsepkov and part of the komandatura's "apparatus," finally landed on the island of Nazino. A zealous Siblag official who had been taught always to report on plans, achievements, and figures, Dolguikh's first concern was to count the number of deportees who had died on the island. He decided that the number of 1,970 dead—all special settlers—reported by the health officers was "grossly exaggerated for obvious political reasons." The Siblag's officials, making a tour of the island guided by a certain Pokorovkii, "a recidivist criminal serving as a nurse responsible for burials," counted the number of common graves. There were thirty-one. They proceeded to exhume and count the bodies in three graves, "one of them exceptionally large, another larger than average, and one smaller one." On the basis of the number of bodies exhumed from each of these graves (55, 22, and 5, respectively), Dolguikh tried to show, in the written report he later submitted to the head of the Siblag, that the number indicated by the

local staff was greatly exaggerated, and emphasized—
and this was the only sensible argument he gave—that
"the gravediggers, all volunteers with criminal back-
grounds, were naturally inclined to inflate the number
of the dead and to include fugitives, because the differentiated and increased rations they received were determined by the number of bodies they had buried, the island's commander not undertaking any verification."[72]

After making this macabre tour, the officials asked to
go to the settlement closest to Nazino, where a group of
deportees had been sent a few weeks earlier. In a small
motorboat, the team traveled up the Nazina some sixty
kilometers to "settlement site no. 1"—not without problems, because once the snow had melted, the level of
river had considerably decreased and sandbanks made
navigation difficult and even impossible. The Siblag leaders and their guards had to travel the last ten kilometers
on foot, through the taiga and the marshes.[73]

Here is the description Dolguikh gave of his visit to "settlement site no. 1," which had been occupied since the
beginning of June by a few hundred survivors from the
island of Nazino:

> A virgin space along the river. A primitive clay oven.
> Rude huts made with pine branches, under which the
> déclassé elements refused to take shelter, preferring to
> gather in the open around wood fires. A single
> wooden hut, which serves as lodging for the com-
> mander and the guards. . . . The contingent consists of
> the most déclassé elements of the cities—truly the re-
> fuse of society. They all proudly advertise the fact that

they come from Moscow or Leningrad. They are all extremely dirty, lice-ridden, emaciated, without shoes, dressed in rags. Some of them are naked. Since they have been there, it is clear that none of them has washed, and despite the fine weather that has now come, none of these elements wants to bathe in the river. When they saw us coming, the déclassés gathered together and began demanding that they be released, each one claiming that he had been exiled here for no good reason. . . . Most of these elements refuse to work, despite the commander's injunctions. "We'd rather die than work," the boldest said openly, "in any case we've been brought here so that we'll die of hunger. We'll run away—that doesn't scare us. We've escaped the Solovki more than once!" I made a speech telling them that those who went to work would get increased rations, along with tobacco and clothing, and eventual liberation as well, while those who refused to work would receive only the minimal rations; as for those who tried to escape, they would be referred to the OGPU's troika. I have to admit that very few reacted positively to my speech. Most of them are incorrigible. The rare individuals who agree to work do so slowly and carelessly.[74]

Dolguikh's speech elicited few "positive reactions," but he was above all interrupted by the seditious shouts already mentioned: "You're starving the people. Well, we're eating one another!" Thereupon the Siblag's high official had his armed guards arrest some fifteen "hotheads."

Back in Nazino, Dolguikh made a series of decisions.

Commander Tsepkov was stripped of his functions and received a "severe censure to be recorded in his personal Party membership file." The leadership of the Alexandro-Vakhovskaia komandatura was entrusted to an official who had come along with Dolguikh's team, a certain Frolov, "a very young and energetic chekist who had been promoted to the rank of commander in 1931, at the age of twenty-two." It was decided to transfer the deportees once again, to new settlement sites near the confluence of the Ob and the Nazina Rivers. The settlement sites chosen by Tsepkov and Suleimanov, which were considerably farther upriver, were no longer accessible by transport boats, the water level having considerably dropped since the end of the thaw, and could therefore no longer be either supplied or supervised. Within one week, the new commander was expected to choose, "with the help of a team of surveyors," new settlement sites at least 15 kilometers away from the confluence of the Ob and the Nazina, and construct settlement villages on them. The déclassé elements transferred to these sites would be subject to a "stricter set of rules that was part of the settlement village plan. "Ringleaders" and "parasites" who refused to work would be arrested and sent before a special OGPU court; a system of "differentiated provisions" would be set up, determined by the work done by each individual (750 grams of bread per day for those who worked, 600 grams for the "weakened," 200 grams for "simulators"). The whole local population would be mobilized—in the framework of the obligatory public labor usually imposed on kolkhozians as well as on special settlers and "indigenous minorities"—in order to construct a landing stage, depots, public baths, and huts. To "increase discipline among the guards," uniforms would be distributed to them. The long list of "decisions"—in reality, a catalogue of intentions for the realization of which the Siblag had no immediate plans to provide funding—concluded with a utopian "prospective economic plan for developing the resources of the Alexandro-Vakhovskaia district in 1933." Before winter arrived, the déclassé elements (a few samples of whom the commission had just seen during its visit to "settlement site no. 1") were supposed to have "cleared 500 hectares and sowed them in rye" and "accumulated sufficient reserves of wood for construction and heating, and of berries, mushrooms, and dried fish for the season when the river is not navigable and resupply by the state is particularly difficult."[75]

After this meeting, Dolguikh and his team left again on board the *Karl Marx*, leaving the new Commander Frolov with the difficult task of implementing the decisions they had made. Frolov, who was very energetic, mobilized all the available forces and succeeded in particular in convincing several economic organizations making use of special settlers to "lend" him for two months three "construction brigades" (about sixty men in all, hardworking dekulakized peasants) to build huts and bread ovens. In a few weeks, a settlement village like those that sheltered the peasants deported to this area in the first two waves of deportation in 1930–31 rose up about 15 kilometers from Nazino. The survivors from "settlement site no. 1," about 250 persons, were installed there around mid-July. However, Frolov did not have time to transfer the approximately 2,000 survivors of the island of Nazino who were living farther upstream in settlement sites numbers 2 through 5. In fact, during the first half of July, he had to deal with the arrival of three additional convoys of déclassé elements (some 4,200 individuals) from the Tomsk transit camp that had been delayed for several weeks following the "Nazino affair."

Since the middle of May, when the first convoys were sent to the Narym region, the transit camps in Tomsk, Omsk, and Achinsk had continued to receive tens of thousands of deportees coming from Ukraine, the North Caucasus, the Volga regions, Moscow, and Leningrad. In all, nearly 100,000 persons. The peasant contingents, which represented more than 80 percent of the total number of deportees, had been distributed among a dozen komandaturas in the Narym region. Because they had generally arrived in poor physical condition, and usually came from regions suffering from famines, the human losses among the peasant deportees in this "third wave" (as officials in the Special Settlements Department called it) were still higher than those of the preceding years.[76] Though precarious, their "installation" nonetheless took place under conditions more or less similar to those of the first two waves. As we have seen, the case was otherwise for the completely deprived urban déclassé elements sent to the Alexandro-Vakhovskaia komandatura. Despite the assurances given by the Gulag's leadership that no further contingents of this type would be sent to Western Siberia,[77] the Tomsk camp received, during the month of June alone, more than 6,000 additional déclassé elements, and as many more in July.[78]

In a dispatch sent to Genrikh Iagoda at the end of July, Alexeiev, the OGPU's plenipotentiary representative for Western Siberia, once again protested against the "sending of large numbers of aged and infirm persons and women with small children of whom Moscow and Leningrad are ridding themselves." "These elements," he added, "have no value in terms of economic development." He cited in particular a convoy of 1,719 deportees that had left Moscow on July 9 and arrived in Tomsk a week later. A very large number of elderly persons had been counted, along with numerous invalids, blind persons, deaf-mutes, and mentally retarded persons. The great majority of the people who arrived "with family" were women alone with small children, "arrested while they were passing through Moscow, despite all the official documents and attestations certifying that these persons had a specific reason to go to the capital."[79] More than 300 deportees in this convoy had to be transferred to the Siblag's dispensaries, hospices, and hospitals, which were already saturated. As for the others, they were to be sent to the Alexandro-Vakhovskaia komandatura. The head of the Siblag wondered what economic benefit the Soviet state would derive from them.

Around the middle of July, the Tomsk camp had also received other convoys from Moscow consisting exclusively of Gypsies (5,470 persons, including 1,440 men, 1,506 women, and 2,524 children) who had been expelled from the capital and the area around it in connection with a vast police operation that had begun on June 28 and was completed on July 3. These "Gypsies without fixed domicile," the assistant head of the Gulag explained, had been authorized to take along with them

338 horses, 2 cows, and a large quantity of miscellaneous objects. All the deportees have undergone disinfection and had their hair cut. . . . . The Gulag has made available to this contingent an adequate quantity of food for humans and livestock, in accord with the administrative norms in force. Each convoy has its own mobile kitchens and a sufficient number of dishes to provide the deportees with hot food and boiling water . . . as well as a quarantine car in the event of an epidemic.[80]

After a brief stop in the Tomsk transit camp, the approximately 5,000 Gypsies were taken by river to "settlement sites" in the Galkinskaia komandatura. At the end of a few weeks, virtually all the Gypsies had fled.[81]

In late July 1933, two additional convoys of "déclassé and socially harmful elements" rounded up in Moscow and Leningrad (nearly 3,000 individuals in all) arrived in the Tomsk transit camp. The report sent on this occasion to Genrikh Iagoda by Pliner, the assistant head of the Gulag and the chief official of the Special Settlements Department, clearly raised the question of the ultimate fate of these groups of outlaws deported to the other end of the country, into veritable "garbage-can zones" from which many of them escaped, thus continually frustrating and discouraging the police forces, for whom the sole result of all these operations seemed to be to "shift criminals from one place to another." In Pliner's view, the "socially harmful elements" must no longer be sent to labor villages, but rather to camps, "in order not to contaminate, through their pernicious, demoralizing influence, other contingents of deportees."[82]

For the time being, Pliner's proposal was shelved. But it was quickly revived as soon as word of the "Nazino affair" reached Stalin himself.

According to the final version of the "Settlement Plan for the New Contingent of Labor Colonists for the Year 1933" worked out in May 1933 by the Siblag leadership, the Alexandro-Vakhovskaia komandatura was to receive a total of at least 20,000 deportees. The "Nazino affair" delayed for several weeks the dispatch of further contingents. However, at the end of June, a new convoy of 1,608 déclassé elements was sent to Alexandrovskoie, this time, it seems, with a minimum of equipment, tools, and provisions for two months. This convoy was followed by two others that left Tomsk on July 14 and July 18. The three convoys were unloaded about a hundred kilometers upstream from Nazino, at the confluence of the Ob and the Pania Rivers. According to reports submitted by Commander Frolov and by Vlassov, the local Party "boss," "the errors committed during the dispatch and reception of the first contingents of déclassés were not repeated."[83] Thus the deportees who arrived in pitiful shape (more than a third of them were "severely emaciated, in rags, and without shoes") at the landing stage in Verkhniaja Pania received "buckwheat soup, 500 grams of bread, and, after two or three days, some dried fish." The places having been equipped with "three public baths," a "complete disinfection of the individuals and their clothing within two to three days of their disembarkation" was undertaken. "Thanks to this perfectly controlled reception," Vlassov reported, "only twenty-three individuals died over the first few days, in addition

to the four who died during transport, most of whom
were elderly people or young vagabonds who were very
emaciated."[84]

At the end of a week, all the deportees were sent by
boat to their "final settlement sites," a few dozen kilometers up the Pania River. Two brigades of carpenters,
composed of deported peasants "lent by the Rybtrest,"
were supposed to help the déclassé elements build huts,
stoves, and bread ovens. However, slightly qualifying his
rosy picture of a "perfectly controlled reception," Vlassov
acknowledged that most of the deportees had refused to
go to work and had tried to escape. Thus in Nekrasovka,
a special village on the banks of the Pania where 340
persons had been installed, hardly ninety participated in
the construction of huts; most of them "spent their time
fishing." One week after their arrival at their "final settlement site," 120 persons had already fled.[85] The short-
age of supervisory personnel and guards further aggravated the general atmosphere of sloppiness. Only ten
guards accompanied the convoy of 1,068 deportees unloaded at Verkhniaja on July 4. The guards had hardly
arrived before they began asking to go back to Tomsk,
refusing to go any further into the taiga "to graze dangerous criminals there." Only the threat of immediate
arrest for desertion got them to remain.[86] A last shadow
in the picture: the persistence of acts of cannibalism. On
July 10, three deportees were arrested while they were
eating human flesh. After running away from Verkhniaja Pania, they had wandered about in the taiga for several days. Encountering another group of fugitives, they
had, by common agreement, sacrificed a "cow." The
other cannibals were not found. "Cannibals roaming the

taiga close to the special villages maintain a tense climate favoring all sorts of anti-Soviet rumors," Vlassov concluded.[87]

These field reports contrasted strongly with the dispatches exchanged at higher levels. For example, the document Gorchkov sent on July 11, 1933 to Matvei Berman—the head of the Gulag, who was passing through Novosobirsk on his way back from a tour to Vladivostok—stated that "the Nazino incident is over," and "the situation under complete control." "The construction of huts, public baths, disinfection rooms, and storehouses is in full swing, as are the distribution of clothing and the stockpiling of provisions for the winter. Most of the special settlers are working hard. The development plans will be carried out."[88]

At the same time that the Party's regional authorities and the Siblag were attempting, by common accord, to minimize and close the "Nazino incident," Velichko, the young journalist-propagandist, was undertaking his own investigation of the situation of the work colonists in the Alexandro-Vakhovskii district. Did he do so on his own initiative, or was the investigation commissioned by the local newspaper for which he also wrote? The answer to this question is not clear. But one thing is certain: the subject of the special settlers was far from being taboo. On the contrary: in a region in which they constituted the majority of the local population, the deportees' "economic successes" and their "transformation into decent and hardworking Soviet citizens" were regular topics of propaganda articles published in the local press. Velichko spent nearly three weeks in the Nazino area. He went not only to the island, but also to the five or six deportee settlement sites along the Nazina River. When he had completed his investigation, he wrote not a propaganda article for the local newspaper, but a long report which he sent simultaneously to his immediate superior, Levits, the secretary of the Party Committee of the Narym region; to Robert Eikhe; and to Stalin himself. This was a bold act on the part of a minor bureaucrat who was only twenty-five years old, but it was not unprecedented. Stalin strongly encouraged "Communists of the base" to send directly to him "signals" regarding what was going on at the local level, bypassing the Party hierarchy; he suspected regional officials of providing Moscow with only partial and embellished information. As a staunch Communist, Velichko obviously did not question the wisdom of deporting kulaks and déclassé elements to the least hospitable areas of the country. He limited himself to denouncing the "series of errors and cases of negligence" that had led "to the stunning collapse of a great project for the colonization of a Siberian region."[89] After describing in detail what happened in the Nazino area, from the deportees' arrival to their evacuation, in a mad panic, to new settlement sites, Velichko analyzed the sequence of events leading to this situation and pinpointed "two political errors" revealed by the facts: the local officials "had absolutely failed to understand what they had to do with the individuals for whom they were responsible," and their "dreadful mismanagement of manpower" had not ended with the island's evacuation, since the settlers had continued to die in great numbers in their new settlement sites. According to Velichko, on August 20 barely 2,200 people remained alive out of the 6,600 to 6,800 who had arrived from Tomsk.[90]

In his report, Velichko devoted a lengthy passage to the unjustified arrest and deportation of "individuals socially close to the Soviet government, and even comrades, most of whom died, because they were the most vulnerable." He described in detail no fewer than thirty cases of individuals who had spontaneously come up to him to tell their stories and ask that he help them get permission to return to Moscow or Leningrad. The journalist-propagandist was the first bureaucrat who had taken the trouble to listen to and transmit their grievances. In his deposition before the commission of inquiry, Commander Frolov explained that Dolguikh had expressly forbidden the komandatura's officials to receive any requests or complaints made by individuals who claimed to have been wrongly deported. If the latter presented a certificate, an attestation, or even identity papers, these documents were to be immediately confiscated. "Such papers could only have been stolen," Frolov said. "One day a deportee came up to me, told me he was a candidate for membership in the Party,[91] and asked me which Communist cell he should put himself down for now. I asked to see his card. He gave it to me. It said that he had paid his dues for the first months of the current year. I took this card to the District Committee of the Party. There I was told, 'This card must have been stolen. Impostors and masked enemies with Party cards in their pockets, they're everywhere.'"[92] The Siblag officials' concern that some deportees might file written complaints had, however, little foundation. As Velichko noted in his report, "Even the komandatura's bureaucrats write their budgets and their accounts on birch bark."[93] A detail that tells us a great deal about material poverty in this remote part of the Soviet world.

Sent from Tomsk, Velichko's long letter (about twenty pages) to Stalin arrived in Moscow at the beginning of September 1933. Stalin ordered that it be circulated among the members of the Politburo. The signatures of Kaganovich, Molotov, Kalinin, Kuybyshev, and Mikoyan appearing at the end of the letter show that the Party's highest officials were aware of the "Nazino affair." On September 23, the Politburo assigned a high official who was a member of the Central Supervisory Commission and an assistant to the People's Commissar for the Inspection of Workers and Peasants to look into the matter.[94] He supervised the establishment of the commission of inquiry headed by Maxim Kovalev to which we have already referred. This commission included officials of the Party, the judiciary, the OGPU, and the Gulag. The commission spent several weeks in the area, evaluating the situation of the special settlers in the komandaturas of the Narym region, checking the justification of the complaints of hundreds of survivors who said they had been deported for no reason, and questioning the main officials, from Commander Tsepkov to the head of the Siblag, about the "Nazino affair."

On the way to Nazino, the commission visited several "settlement villages," all of them in a terrible state of dilapidation that contrasted with official reports. In Beriozovka, out of a group of 682 deportees (185 men, 213 women, 284 children) who had arrived from Tomsk two weeks earlier, 58 had already died.[95] The situation was even worse in the "settlement sites" along the Nazina River, where the survivors of "Death Island" had been transferred. According to the commission's final report,

> The huts are half-buried. A roof made of branches through which the autumn rains pour. No windows. Inside, rows of pallets, with a little dry grass to serve as a blanket. Half-naked, emaciated, dirty, lice-ridden individuals lying there. Outside the huts, the more vigorous ones warm themselves around wood fires. . . . When the local commander was asked, "Why do the deportees stay outside?" he replied: "All the dé-classés are used to living around wood fires. They've always done that. They do it here, too." We also went to the huts into which had been crowded people suffering from dysentery, tuberculosis, scurvy, and syphilis, along with severely emaciated individuals. They were all lying on pallets, covered with a blanket of grass that hadn't been changed for weeks and that emitted a pestilential odor of manure. When we asked, "Why are these individuals in such a state?" we were told that they had always been sick and emaciated and that in any case they could not be cared for because there was a lack of everything. . . . We estimated that there were at least 800 bedridden sick people. . . . A few rare able-bodied individuals were constantly bustling about building huts. At one settlement site, the commission noticed a piece of land that had been cleared and sown, about one hectare in area.[96]

During its inspection tour, the commission severely criticized the local officials of the Party and the komandaturas, whom it accused of "a loss of class feeling" and "moral and political degeneracy." It suggested that this resulted from "prolonged isolation in a hostile environment." Its report emphasized that "the Communists in the Narym region prefer hunting bears to assiduously reading the Party's newspapers."[97] In addition to inspecting the deportees' "settlement sites," the commission was supposed to check the foundation for the complaints filed by hundreds of persons who claimed that they had been unjustly deported. In the course of three weeks spent in the area, the commission's members personally questioned 810 individuals. Of this number, 174 were freed of their status as labor colonists and sent back to Tomsk or Novosibirsk—without, however, being authorized to go home, at least until a more detailed investigation of their cases had been made; 231 were sent to Novosibirsk under escort for further investigation; the cases of 240 others were referred to a long and aleatory bureaucratic control procedure that passed through the Siblag's usual channels, and 165 were rejected.[98] These figures clearly show that in most of the cases examined, the commission members acknowledged, more or less explicitly, that in most of the protests and challenges were well-founded. However, none of the persons wrongly deported was allowed to go home. And, of course, no compensation or indemnification of any kind was envisaged.

Finally, the commission attempted to determine the number of survivors and to draw up a balance sheet for the operation of "colonization" begun several months earlier. In mid-October, of the 10,289 persons deported to the Alexandro-Vakhovskaia komandatura,[99] there remained on site only 2,025. In mid-September, shortly before the commission's arrival, 1,940 of the more able-bodied deportees had been transferred to the Siblag's labor camps.[100] Thus in this district alone, almost two-thirds of the contingent of deportees—6,324 persons—had disappeared since the beginning of the deportation campaign in 1933. This was the conclusion drawn by the Kovalev Commission, and based, as the authors of the report noted, not without reservations, on "the figures that we were able to obtain from the local authorities."[101] Nevertheless, no matter how imprecise these figures may be,[102] their general magnitude is very eloquent. The commission estimated the state of the 2,000 survivors as follows: 50 percent ill and bedridden, 35–40 percent in weakened condition, 10–15 percent—or about 200–300 persons—capable of working.[103]

Back in Alexandrovskoie, on October 18, Kovalev telegraphed his initial conclusions to Matvei Berman, the head of the Gulag. It emerged that "in order to avoid further deterioration of the situation of the special settlers who are still alive," there was henceforth no solution other than to "rapidly reexamine the cases of the survivors, [to] let the least socially dangerous ones leave, forbidding them to reside in cities subject to special rules, to send the more dangerous ones back to the Tomsk camp, at least until spring, and to completely evacuate all the sites where the deportees in the 1933 contingent had been installed."[104] These proposals were in fact similar to those made a few weeks earlier by Alexeiev, after the most able-bodied deportees had been transferred to a labor camp.[105] This transfer, which all the Siblag's officials had been requesting for months, confirmed the failure of the great plan for the colonization of the Siberian vastnesses by urban déclassé elements that had been proposed by Genrikh Iagoda six months earlier.

The commission submitted its report on October 31. It acknowledged that "essentially, the facts mentioned by comrade Velichko in his letter to J. V. Stalin were correct." However, the proposals formulated two weeks earlier by Kovalev, the commission's chairman, regarding the ultimate fate of the survivors of the Alexandro-Vakhovskaia komandatura were not included in the final text. Obviously, no one had wanted to take responsibility for a new transfer of deportees to Tomsk. The city's authorities refused to accept any new influx of déclassé elements. As for the transit camp, it was "completely saturated," with 8,000 deportees whom it had not been possible to send on to one of the komandaturas of the Narym region having to spend the winter there. The season when the river was navigable was coming to an end, and the Rechtrans was bringing in its boats. The *Karl Marx* had just completed its last Tomsk–Alexandrovskoie–Tomsk run. It was no longer possible to evacuate the survivors of Nazino to more hospitable places.

The commission limited itself to expressing the hope that the Siblag would continue to "take all measures that might improve living conditions for the special settlers," emphasizing that "at the time of [our] departure, local officials were actively trying to respond to the commission's demands concerning the dispatch of medicines, clothing, and provisions that would allow the special settlers to live a normal life on site until spring."[106]

On November 1, the highest regional political authority, the Office of the Regional Committee of the Party of Western Siberia, headed by Robert Eikhe, met to discuss the commission's report. The resolution adopted at the conclusion of the meeting was essentially devoted to the declaration of sanctions imposed on about ten Siblag officials who had been in some way involved in the "Nazino affair." Gorchkov and Dolguikh received "severe reprimands"—which did not prevent them from pursuing their brilliant careers in the Gulag's bureaucracy; Dolguikh ended his career as head of the Gulag in the early 1950s. The minor local officials were the most severely sanctioned: not only Tsepkov, Kolubaiev, and Kuznetsov, but also Frolov were expelled from the Party, arrested, and sent before the College of the OGPU, an extrajudicial panel authorized to punish crimes and offenses committed by chekists. They were sentenced to terms of one to three years in a camp for having "sabotaged the implementation of the State's 1933 plan for colonizing the Narym region." Finally, about fifteen village commanders and guards who had committed particularly serious "abuses" with regard to the special settlers (murders, blows, and injuries) were sent before an internal OGPU disciplinary panel.[107]

In addition, the Office of the Regional Committee of the Party of Western Siberia acknowledged that "the contingents of déclassé deportees were completely unsuited for colonizing the Siberian Great North," and exhorted the Party's Central Committee not to send any further contingents of this kind to Western Siberia. Finally, the OGPU's plenipotentiary representative was requested to "examine the question of the grounds for the continuing presence of déclassé elements in the Alexandro-Vakhovskaia komandatura, with a view to definitively evacuating them to other sites."[108]

With this tortuous formulation, which reflects the dead end at which the "grandiose plan" for using special settlers and "labor colonists" to develop the inhospitable regions of the USSR had arrived, the "Nazino affair" came to an end.

Conclusion

The "Cannibal Island" episode is exceptionally well documented in comparison with other mass deportations. What can we learn from it? First of all, it sheds light on the bloody implementation of a utopia—a vast enterprise of social engineering, of bureaucratic and police planning, that sought to "cleanse" and "purify" certain Soviet spaces—notably urban spaces—of their "déclassé and socially harmful elements" by deporting them to Siberia's "garbage-can" areas. It also allows us to understand better the functioning, about which we still know little, of the system of "special settlements," the "second Gulag," that developed and prospered for a quarter of a century alongside the system of labor camps. The Nazino affair, which reveals the climate of extreme violence that overcame the Soviet "Far East" in the early 1930s, also suggests what happened in largely unsupervised areas on the Soviet periphery and the level of violence that reigned in them. Finally, it constitutes a remarkable laboratory for the anthropological observation of a group of individuals plunged into an extreme situation that generated regressions and transgression as the end result of a veritable process of decivilization.[1]

The "grandiose plan" proposed in early 1933 by officials of the political police and approved by Stalin was the natural extension—a second, still more comprehensive stage—of a project begun three years earlier, and for the most part completed: the "liquidation of the kulaks as a class." The project launched at the beginning of 1930 had a twofold objective: to "extract"—that was the term used in the confidential directives—the elements that might resist the forced collectivization of the countryside, and to colonize the vast, inhospitable areas of Siberia, the Great North, the Urals, and Kazakhstan. The first objective responded to the vision, clearly expressed by the Bolsheviks as soon as they came to power, according to which peasant society, which was shot through with class antagonisms, contained "elements" irremediably hostile to the regime. The second objective was part of a vast plan to develop, by means of deported manpower, a certain number of deserted regions, at a point when the regime was throwing itself into "the construction of socialism." These objectives were based on the conviction that the new state, because it was based on scientific knowledge and the mastery of the laws governing the historical development of societies, was capable of shaping the latter, of excising from them hostile, parasitical, or harmful elements that were "polluting" the new socialist society that was being built.

In this social engineering, "the number culture" that had invaded the most diverse domains of political life played a central role, producing "dekulakization quotas," detailed plans for the eradication of malaria, curves for ending illiteracy, and five-year production targets. This is shown by the dekulakization quotas assigned to each region in 1930–31[2] and the countless deportation plans worked up by various departments of "accounting and monitoring" in the OGPU's central Special Settlements Office. The obsession with numbers is discernible in all the sources on which this book is based. Overall numbers planned in Moscow, numbers "negotiated" by local authorities, statistical plans of "déclassé elements to be settled" sent to the local leaders of the komandaturas, the "percentage of emaciated or lice-ridden individuals" put into the deportation convoys, "records broken" (the head of Special Settlements for Western Siberia proudly announced that in 65–70 days they had succeeded in colonizing the Narym region, which the Czarist regime had not been able to do in three hundred and fifty years)—the omnipresent, invasive number culture is the mark of a utopian mastery over the body social, broken down into deindividualized "masses to be processed," to adopt a vocabulary used by both the decision makers and the executors of the various deportation projects.

Along with this number culture emerged a veritable "planning esthetics"[3] perceptible, in the area that concerns us here, in the utopian goal of creating a perfectly ordered system of settlement colonies and special villages managed in a military-repressive way. Bureaucratic records are full of plans, schemes, and projects showing how the experimental special villages were supposed ideally to function, with their model, standardized huts, their "disinfection stations" (the obsession with hygiene is found everywhere), their punctilious internal regulations, which determined even the kind of literature that would be distributed to the deportees, and their structures of surveillance, regimentation, and reeducation through labor.[4] In the initial stage of the "Great Turning Point," the special village or settlement colony was even considered a possible substitute for the camp, as is shown by the astonishing project elaborated in April 1930 by the head of the OGPU, Genrikh Iagoda:

> The question of the camps must be reconsidered. Today, a camp is nothing but a conglomeration of detainees whose labor power we exploit from day to day, but that offers no long-term prospects either for us or for the detainees. The camps must be transformed into settlement colonies. . . . Here is my idea: transform all the detainees into colonists. We should proceed this way: We assign to a specific group of detainees (let's say, 1,500 persons) a small area of forest, and we have them construct shelters to live in. Those who want to will be able to have their families join them. Each village will be run by an official. A village will consist of 200 to 300 families. When they have finished their woodcutting work, they can work in their vegetable gardens, raise pigs, mow fields, go fishing. At first, we will provide them with food, but soon they will get along by themselves. Deportees and exiles will be treated like the detainees—that is, they will be transformed into colonists. In winter, all the colonists will work at cutting wood or other kinds of labor, depending on the orders we have given them. The regions to be colonized are immensely rich in oil and in coal, and I am convinced that within a few years we can make these settlement colonies into real proletarian cities.[5]

The third part of this utopia was a pseudocategorization of the stigmatized groups to be expelled from the countryside or the cities and deported. These groups were to be put in a camp after being subjected to an extrajudicial administrative procedure or simply rounded up by the police. The explosive combination of plans specifying numerical targets and a totally arbitrary categorization of the victims—a categorization whose interpretation was left to local police officials (or even, in the case of the dekulakization campaign, ordinary neighbors seeking to settle old scores)—could only lead to the most complete arbitrariness.

Thus far from being the planned operation based on "clear objectives" and "controlled quotas" that the OGPU's leaders dreamed of, dekulakization turned into a chaotic and largely unmonitored process. In their internal reports, the leaders of the political police constantly complained about the local authorities, whom they accused of not arresting "those who should be arrested"—which was hardly surprising, since no one had ever defined exactly what a "kulak" was.[6] The same scenario was repeated in 1933, the inflation of the pseudocategories of "déclassé" and "socially harmful" elements naturally allowing absolutely arbitrary interpretations of what they meant. Still more than other roundups and deportations that took place in the spring of 1933—regarding which we unfortunately have only very fragmentary information—the "Nazino affair" permits us to gain greater insight into this environment and the arbitrary police actions that took place in it. To "meet the targets and provide the resulting figures," police officials did not hesitate to arrest and deport the elderly, the ill, mothers with young children, and other "ordinary" citizens whose only offense was to have left home without their papers or to have "raised their voices." In turn, these cases of the "dizziness of success" and "administrative enthusiasm"—to adopt some of Stalin's favorite formulas—set in motion a whole mechanism of bureaucratic oversight and verification. However, the latter's goal was not to redress an injustice or reestablish a kind of legality, but rather to provide a political explanation for the great utopian projects of "developing" inhospitable territories and for the system's malfunctions.

The "Nazino affair" sheds light on these malfunctions, the bureaucratic relationship between the Center and the periphery, and the various actors involved in the special settlements system. In the outline of a "rational" and hierarchical categorization of Soviet territories—the goal of the great campaign of passportization and deportation in 1933[7]—Siberia, the Great North, and Kazakhstan were seen as "garbage-can areas" into which all the elements polluting socialism's showcase cities, Moscow, Leningrad, and other large cities "subject to special rules" would be dumped. For Siberian political officials, the influx of hundreds of thousands of social pariahs (a significant number of whom escaped any supervision after they arrived) had, as the OGPU's plenipotentiary representative for Western Siberia bluntly explained, "zero value in terms of economic exploitation and development," and was a major source of social disorder and insecurity. For his part, Robert Eikhe, the chief Party official for Siberia, believed that "In no area is the gap between the Center and the periphery so great as in matters concerning the special settlers." On the one hand, there was a tendency to "manipulate the numbers, to elaborate grandiose plans," and on the other, an obligation "to install masses of people in the taiga, in record time and without material support, and to prevent them from escaping." Whence the incessant bargaining (in which the regions, it has to be admitted, had little room for maneuver), a total absence of coordination among the countless bureaucracies involved in policing and managing the deportees, contradictory instructions, constant setbacks—and all of this aggravated by the remoteness of the areas concerned and the lamentable state of communications. If we add to these structural factors the high-pressure temporal imperative—the massive deportations of 1933 had to be carried out in only two to three months, weather constraints playing a major role—we have all the ingredients allowing us to understand the chain of events that led to the fatal "deportation and abandonment" on the island of Nazino. Thanks to the documents produced by the commission of inquiry set up at that time, we can now also understand the role played by the officials involved at all levels, their degree of autonomy and their way of interpreting and implementing the project worked out in Moscow. It is clear that these officials had only a vague notion of the project's goal. For the most part, they were confused by orders and plans that were constantly changing (25,000 deportees to be settled in such and such a komandatura, then 15,000, then 5,000), and didn't know what to do with the "contingents of urban déclassés" for which they were responsible: should they always be sent somewhere else? "Put out to graze"? Or "finished off"?—to adopt a few of the blunt expressions used by the Siblag's lower-echelon personnel. In the eyes of the people implementing the project at the base level, wasn't the

generalized carelessness that accompanied the whole enterprise, from Moscow down to Alexandrovskoie, the
strongest possible incentive to physically eliminate these
"elements," who appeared, moreover, to be so alien?

The story of Nazino has a third aspect: what it tells us
about these remote, immense, and violent areas that
constituted the Soviet "Far East." They were insecure areas poorly controlled by the authorities, where marginal
elements and outlaws were concentrated, where armed
gangs attacked isolated kolkhozes and killed the few
"representatives of the Soviet government," where everyone was armed, where human life had scarcely any
value, and where humans rather than animals were
sometimes hunted. Since the beginning of the 1930s, as
a result of the destruction of the Siberian peasantry,
which was no doubt the most enterprising in all Russia,
this area had been overcome by extreme poverty, shortages, and hunger that raised still higher the level of ambient violence. These were areas where the state in the
sense defined by Max Weber—"a system that successfully claims the right to rule a territory by virtue of its
monopoly on the use of legitimate physical violence"[8]—
was virtually absent.

It was into this explosive cauldron that hundreds of
thousands of outlaws were deported. Should we be sur-
prised that every year one-third of these deportees died
or escaped? This rate of loss seems not to have much
disturbed the decision makers, who regarded it as not
particularly high in view of the exceptional scope of the
enterprise undertaken—an enterprise that was part of
the "Party line," and to which one had therefore to ad-

here, no matter what doubts might be expressed by this or that local official. In Nazino, as the result of a set of aggravating circumstances (a group of exceptionally deprived and ill-suited individuals sent without the slightest supervision and unloaded in particularly inhospitable places), two-thirds of the deportees vanished in a few weeks. This bloody episode is an extreme, limiting case that took place not only as part of the implementation of a utopia, of the functioning of a bureaucratic and repressive system—that of the special settlements—but also in an area saturated with violence.

"On the island of Nazino, people ceased to be people. They turned into jackals," wrote the journalist-propagandist Velichko in his letter to Stalin—probably unaware that he was paraphrasing the famous *Homo homini lupus*. This leads us to a fourth aspect of the episode of "Cannibal Island" that we have hardly touched upon so far, largely because of the specific character of the sources used here, which are more suitable for an account of bureaucratic malfunctions: Nazino was also a place of decivilization. Decivilization on the level of material culture, the most striking evidence for which is the resurgence of the very ancient practice of writing on birch bark, still attested in the medieval Rus'. Decivilization as well on the level of human relationships: too few in number, but extremely revelatory, the statements and acts of the "representatives of the Soviet government"— local officials of the Party and the Siblag's komandaturas, and other guardians responsible for monitoring the deportees and keeping them under surveillance—lay bare extremely violent relationships based on transforming the deportees into animals. In Nazino, we see the resuscitation of a pastoral order from the earliest times: guardian-shepherds grazing their animals, beating them for the slightest offense, training them to row and to retrieve game. Those who refused to comply with this order or tried to escape were hunted like wild animals, gunned down as dangerous and bestial predators who ate human flesh. In Nazino, a modernizing utopia of purifying and civilizing social engineering under complete control paradoxically caused a whole nest of archaisms to rise to the surface. In this sense, this episode mirrored the Stalinist vision—and its reality—as a whole.[9]

Epilogue, 1933–37

The approximately 4,000 people who disappeared in Nazino represented at most 1 percent of the total number of deportees who vanished in 1933. According to the centralized statistics of the head Office of Special Settlements, 367,457 special settlers disappeared that year, or one-third of the total number recorded on January 1, 1933.[1] Out of the 367,457 who disappeared, 151,601 were recorded as dead, 215,856 as "fugitives."[2] The extreme precision of these figures, like the differentiation between deportees who died and those who were fugitives, must be taken with a grain of salt when we discover what really happened to the special settlers and the way in which the OGPU's accounting departments functioned. However, the general magnitude of the numbers remains, along with the hundreds of confidential reports exchanged among OGPU directors—all of which describe a terrifying situation in the labor villages of Siberia, the Urals, the North, and Kazakhstan decimated by epidemics, shortages, and famines.[3]

In a document from March 1933 describing the situation in the labor villages of the Archangelsk region, we read:

The special settlers eat all sorts of substitutes—roots, grasses, dogs, cats, carcasses of various kinds—and this leads to high mortality rates and to a swelling of the body characteristic of alimentary dystrophy. Constantly looking for food, special settlers commit numerous thefts in the neighboring kolkhozes, which causes a perceptible increase in the number of lynchings of thieves by the peasants. As a result of acute food-supply problems, the special settlers' productivity has greatly decreased. Emaciated, they are no longer able to meet the targets, and therefore they receive less food and continue to weaken until they are no longer capable of working at all, after which they die of hunger and exhaustion. The outcome is that none of the economic objectives has been realized, and all the plans for the current year are seriously compromised.[4]

The starting point for the fatal series of events described in this report was the drastic decrease—on the order of 50 to 70 percent—of all the supply norms prescribed for the special settlers over the first half of 1933. Genrikh Iagoda's great deportation plan served as a pretext for this brutal "readjustment of the available resources" in the context of a grave economic crisis.[5]

In reality, the "grandiose plan" of deportation "realized" its initial objectives only at the rate of 13.4 percent. In the project Iagoda presented to Stalin in February 1933, two million persons were to be deported. In March, the Politburo approved a plan that cut this figure in half. Ultimately, 268,000 persons were actually deported in the course of 1933, 132,000 of them to Western Siberia.[6] In the meantime, Stalin, in one of the sudden reversals to which he was given, had decided to apply the brakes to a process that was threatening to get out of hand without producing, amid the surrounding disorder, convincing economic results with regard to the use of manpower and the development of inhospitable regions. On May 8, 1933, a secret directive sent to all the regional leaders of the Party, of the political police, and of the legal system condemned the "abuses" committed in recent months and, in accord with a well-tested and familiar method, put the responsibility for the "cases of excessive repression" on local officials. The directive called for an "immediate cessation of large-scale deportations of peasants," with the exception of a "residual quota of 12,000 kulak families (48,000 individuals)", and for the "decongestion of places of detention."[7] After this directive was issued, the "deportation objectives" were reduced to 600,000, then to 425,000 individuals. The number of targeted categories was also reduced from six to four (kulaks and "detainees serving sentences from three to five years in prison").[8] In contrast to Iagoda's original plan, the deportation to labor villages of "urban déclassé elements" and "urban elements refusing to leave the cities in the context of passportization operations" was no longer explicitly envisaged. As we have seen, these new directives had hardly any effect on police practices: all through the summer of 1933, thousands of persons labeled déclassés or socially harmful continued to be rounded up and sent, without further ado, to Siberia or Kazakhstan. But the new directives did further disrupt the already complex processes of management and supervision connected with the mass deportations.

When the country's leaders learned about the "Nazino

affair" in this particular context, it played a major role in discrediting the system of special settlements and the great projects for using urban déclassé elements to colonize the undeveloped expanses of Siberia and Kazakhstan. This was not so much because of the number of victims—on the scale of the overall demographic losses of 1933, the four thousand people who disappeared from Nazino were insignificant in the decision makers' eyes—as because this episode brought to light all the dysfunctions of the special settlements and their economic bankruptcy. Starting in the second half of 1933, the growth of the number of special settlements—which had up to that time been extremely rapid—was abruptly halted. No further large-scale deportations took place for several years,[9] and the number of special settlers continued to decrease regularly until the beginning of World War II.[10] Conversely, starting in 1933 the population of labor camps sharply increased: in that year, the number of detainees rose by more than 50 percent[11] and crossed the threshold of half a million. Four years later, the Gulag's camps already held a million prisoners.[12] The 1933 famine in the special settlements and the "Nazino affair" made a decisive contribution to the shift in the Gulag system's center of gravity toward the labor camps. At the same time, the completion of the first pharaonic construction project carried out using detainees—more than a hundred thousand of them—the White Sea–Baltic Canal, convinced political and police leaders that the camps were more "economically efficacious" than the special settlements.

Nonetheless, the "Nazino affair" did not put an end to the policy of "cleansing" the cities—and particularly

cities subject to special rules—of their déclassé and socially harmful elements. In one year (August 1933–
August 1934), in connection with the passportization of
the urban population, half a million "socially harmful
elements," "parasites," and "criminals" were arrested
and expelled from the cities or sent to labor camps after
a summary procedure carried out by police commissions.[13] Starting in summer 1934, the OGPU and the police embarked upon a broad campaign against "speculators." As the authorities used it, the term "speculation"
included any resale of products in short supply, as well
as the countless kinds of small-scale trafficking engaged
in by a marginal population consisting mainly of former
small businessmen and craftsmen who had gone bank-
rupt since the end of the NEP. An increasing number of
roundups were made in markets and train stations; in a
few months, in the cities "subject to special rules" alone,
more than 60,000 "speculators" were arrested and sentenced to terms in the camps, and 50,000 more, who
had been arrested solely on the ground that they were
not engaged in "any socially useful work and were hang-
ing around the markets," were expelled.[14] At the beginning of 1935, Genrikh Iagoda and Andrei Vyshinski, the
USSR's general prosecutor, sent Stalin a project setting
up new police commissions[15] authorized to sentence by
administrative order "hardened violators of the passport
regulations" and, more generally, all socially harmful elements, to a term of up to five years in the camps. These
extrajudicial police commissions (*militseiski troiki*) were
supposed to make possible an "ultra-rapid cleansing of
the cities of all individuals for whom there are no legal
grounds for bringing their cases before a court," cyni-

cally explained the USSR's general prosecutor. On the note accompanying the project, Stalin scrawled: "An ultra-rapid cleansing is useless. We have to clean up gradually and deeply, without hitches or superfluous administrative enthusiasm. As for the rest, I agree."[16] These new police commissions were set up in May 1935. Within two years, they had sentenced more than 300,000 socially harmful elements.[17] These included individuals who had already been sentenced for crimes or who had been arrested for criminal activities and "continued to maintain relationships with the criminal milieu," "professional" beggars and vagabonds, individuals who "have been neither sentenced nor arrested, but are not engaged in socially useful work, have no fixed domicile, or maintain relationships with the criminal milieu," deportees, exiles, and people who had been expelled and had left without justification the place of residence assigned to them, and "people who have repeatedly violated the passport regulations."[18]

Since the beginning of the 1930s—and a fortiori in relation to the 1924 law defining "social dangerousness"—the category of the "socially harmful" underwent a spectacular expansion, as did the severity of the penalties associated with it—as a rule, five years in a labor camp. In the mid-1930s, several new categories—notably, "hooligans" and young vagabonds—further expanded the vast nebula of socially harmful elements. Among the latter, the largest group—more than 600,000 persons—and the most dangerous, according to the authorities, consisted of "ex-kulaks" and "criminals" deported between 1930 and 1933 who had fled their assigned place of residence. Living on the margins of society, with neither papers nor legal status, some of these had ended up finding work in the mines (particularly in the Kuzbass in Western Siberia) and on major construction sites, where the continual lack of manpower made recruiters not very particular about the identity of the people they hired. Others had joined a criminal underworld very specific to the 1930s, halfway between political crime and ordinary crime. Despite the constant growth in the numbers of police officers, crime remained endemic, especially in the Urals and in Siberia, the main regions to which deportees were sent and where the concentration of marginal people was greatest.[19] In the mid-1930s, the Siberian cities of Tomsk, Novokuznetzk, Novosibirsk, Omsk, and Kemerovo were always on the list of the Soviet cities most dangerous from the point of view of criminality.

From 1937 on, the police authorities' perception of marginal and socially harmful groups underwent a significant change. In a context of increasing international tensions, these groups were more and more clearly seen as "insurrectional reservoirs," as elements likely to join a mythical "fifth column of deviationists and saboteurs operating in connection with the secret services of foreign powers."[20] The NKVD made an increasing number of "discoveries" of alleged "insurrectional organizations"—the "General Russian Military Union" based in Siberia and working for the Japanese secret service, the "Polish Military Organization" based in western Ukraine, and so on. NKVD leaders explained in their reports that these organizations, recruiting among the ex-kulaks and criminal elements, were preparing "insurrections" coordinated with an attack, considered imminent, to be made by foreign powers. In May 1937 the head of the NKVD in Western Siberia, Sergei Mironov, sent Robert Eikhe a particularly alarming report concerning the threat represented by "the 208,400 special settlers who have settled in Siberia, a veritable reserve army for the Japanese."[21] In June 1937 the Politburo several times discussed the danger constituted by large concentrations of special settlers in the Urals, the Soviet Far East, and in Siberia. For Stalin and the highest Party leaders, a still more radical cleansing needed to be undertaken. On July 3, Stalin sent the regional leaders of the Party and the NKVD a secret circular ordering them to submit within five days "an estimate of the number of ex-kulaks and criminal elements whom they consider it necessary to arrest by administrative measure, and after a rapid passage before a troika,[22] execute, along with an estimate of the number of less active kulaks and criminal elements who should be arrested and exiled."[23] Over the following days, the regional leaders sent Moscow their preliminary estimates, which were based, it seems, on the number of socially harmful elements whom the local political police and ordinary police already had on file. On July 30, Nikolay Yezhov, the head of the NKVD, signed "NKVD operational order no. 00447 regarding the repression of ex-kulaks, criminals, and other anti-Soviet elements." This document enumerated no less than seven categories (with very fluid contours, as usual) of individuals to be repressed: "ex-kulaks who have participated in a criminal or anti-Soviet group; former members of non-Bolshevist parties, former government officials or Czarist police officers; anti-Soviet elements who have previously served in White, Cossack, or clerical groups; anti-Soviet elements particularly active among the ex-kulaks, the Whites, criminals, members of sects, members of the clergy; criminals (bandits, thieves, recidivists, professional smugglers, cattle and horse thieves) continuing to maintain ties with the criminal world; criminal elements exiled or held in a labor camp and who continue to carry on a criminal activity." All these socially harmful elements were supposed to be divided into two categories: the "more active" and the "less active, but nonetheless hostile." The individuals classed in the first category were to be "immediately arrested, and, after appearing before a troika, shot." Individuals classed in the second category were to be "arrested and sentenced by the troika to a term of eight to ten years in a camp." Order 00447 then presented the quotas, region by region, for the number of individuals to be repressed in the first or second categories." These figures corresponded more or less to the estimates sent in over the preceding weeks by the regional leaders of the Party and the NKVD. In all, the quotas set by order no. 00447 were 76,000 in the first category and 193,000 in the second category. The highest quotas were assigned to the regions of Moscow and Leningrad and to all the regions where there was a high concentration of deportees and marginal groups, with Siberia at the top of the list, followed by the Urals and the Azov-Black Sea region.[24] "Operation no. 00447" was planned to last four months; in fact, it lasted fifteen. The initial quotas for "second-category individuals to be repressed" were doubled, while those for "first-category individuals" were quintupled. In all, 767,000 people were arrested in connection with "operation 00447," and 387,000 of them were shot.[25]

This operation—the largest of about a dozen "large-scale repressive operations" launched by the NKVD between August 1937 and November 1938, a period which has gone down in history as "The Great Terror" and during which more than a million and a half persons were arrested and 800,000 were shot after a summary extra-judicial procedure[26]—constituted the culmination of a whole series of campaigns and police practices that had been undertaken for years and had become increasingly radical. In this process of bloody radicalization, the "Nazino affair" represented, as we have seen, a major milestone.

As Nikolay Yezhov emphasized in the preamble to order no. 00447, the time had come to "eliminate once and for all the entirety of the socially harmful elements who are sapping the foundations of the Soviet state." The individuals to be definitively eradicated included "those who are hiding in rural areas . . . those who have fled special settlements . . . and those who have succeeded in infiltrating cities, companies, transportation, and large construction projects."[27] For the NKVD's bosses, operation no. 00447 was obviously a natural extension of the campaigns of "social cleansing" carried out over the preceding years. Commenting on the way in which this order was presented to the NKVD's agents, a regional official explained that "the basic instructions were to produce as many cases as possible, as quickly as possible, and to formulate them as simply as possible. In particular, everyone who had recently been arrested by the police, even if he had committed no crime, had to be included in the quotas. . . . The point was to complete the work already undertaken and to definitively cleanse the country of all its socially harmful elements."[28]

In many respects, Western Siberia proved to be "exemplary" from the point of view of the implementation of operation no. 00447. The initial quotas assigned to this garbage-can region to which hundreds of thousands of ex-kulaks, déclassés, and socially harmful elements had been deported since 1930 were already among the highest: 6,000 for the "first category," and 14,500 for the "second category." At the energetic urging of Sergei Mironov and Grigorii Gorbatch, the regional heads of the NKVD,[29] the initial quotas for arrests were rapidly expanded. "Thanks to Stakhanovist work," Gorbatch wrote to Yezhov only a few days after the beginning of operation no. 00447,

> within one week we have arrested 3,008 first-category individuals. The quota assigned to the Omsk region—1,000 first-category individuals—has been pulverized. In the first stage, we arrested all the criminals and socially harmful elements already in our files, and then we added those who were in prison but had not yet been sentenced. We are now going to organize, as long as the rivers remain navigable, roundups of fugitive ex-kulaks hiding along the Ob. As for ex-kulaks and other criminals installed in special settlements far from the river routes, I propose to hunt down these elements starting in November, when the marshes will be frozen and we can easily send in operational groups.[30]

A week later, on August 15, Gorbatch sent Yezhov another telegram: "As of August 13, we have arrested 5,444 individuals for the province of Omsk. I request a supplementary quota of 8,000 for the first category."[31] Five days later, Stalin put his handwritten decision on Gorbatch's request: "Approve an increase of the quota by 8,000." This "overrun" was the first of a long series of "supplementary quotas" accorded by Stalin and Yezhov.

In turn, Robert Eikhe, the Party's regional secretary for Western Siberia, asked on September 20 for an additional quota of 3,000 "first-category elements," which was also accorded. The prisons being overcrowded, and the establishment of new camps (provided for in order no. 00447) encountering the usual bureaucratic delays, the easiest solution was to accelerate the procedures still further and increase the proportion of individuals to be executed. By the beginning of October 1937, in Western Siberia alone more than 35,000 persons had been arrested in connection with operation no. 00447, 23,000 of them in the "first category." Of these, more than 19,000 had already been executed.[32] The operation was prepared and carried out like a military expedition against "internal enemies." In each district, an "operational group" including NKVD agents, part of the police officers in the "workers' and peasants' militia,"[33] and even a few Party members was assigned a quota of individuals to arrest. In general, these initial quotas had been set on the basis of lists of individuals already in NKVD or police files (following sentencing or even just arrest), and also on the basis of tax or census lists (particular targets were all those who were in some way "ex-": ex-landlords, ex–Czarist officials, ex-kulaks, ex-members of non-Bolshevist political parties, etc.). When they ran short of individuals to fill the quotas, which rose higher and higher as a dynamics of overruns and competition took hold under the combined effect of incentives from Moscow and the "excess zeal" of local officials, the NKVD and the ordinary police organized, in accord with a method in use for years, roundups in train stations and markets, places frequented by a whole marginal population that was often in violation of one or more of the countless laws penalizing speculation, begging, or "parasitism."[34] However, in deportation areas like Siberia, special settlers constituted the greatest reservoir of enemies. The ex-kulaks and déclassé elements deported in the early 1930s were privileged targets, and the labor villages provided an inexhaustible hunting ground.

The great majority of the approximately 50,000 persons executed and the 30,000 sent to the Gulag in connection with the "operations of mass repression" conducted in Western Siberia between August 1937 and November 1938 belonged to the marginalized group of special settlers, ex-kulaks, and déclassé elements from the cities.[35] In 1937–38, this whole region became one of the largest "dead-man's islands" in the Soviet archipelago.

Acknowledgments

I would like to thank first my colleague at the Institute of History at the Novosibirsk Academy of Sciences, Sergei Krasilnikov, who first drew my attention to the "Nazino affair" some ten years ago and afterward generously kept me informed of advances in research on this episode, sending me, from his remote post, news clippings and photocopies.

I also thank Tatiana Golychkina, an archivist at TsA FSB, for her courteous welcome and her advice.

I owe a special debt to my colleague and friend Christian Ingrao, who always made himself astonishingly available to help, offering me his advice, chapter by chapter, suggesting further reading, and encouraging me when I had doubts about the project.

Thanks too to Catherine Goussef for her attentive rereading and her very helpful comments, which were both friendly and demanding; to Henry Rousso, Stéphane Audoin-Rouzeau, Annette Becker, and Christian Delage, for their comments, criticisms, and advice.

Finally, I thank Evelyne and Maia, my first readers, for their help, their patience, and their support.

Notes

PREFACE

1. A special store owned by the state that dealt in currencies and precious metals. It sold products "in short supply."

2. The *zemlianki* was an extremely rudimentary shelter that was commonly found during the 1930s on five-year plan construction sites and in "new cities." It consisted of a simple trench dug in the earth, roughly sheathed and slightly raised with wooden planks or other materials, and roofed with cut branches.

3. The testimony of Taissa Mikhailovna Chokareva and Maria Nikitichna Akhtina, of the Khanty ethnic group (born 1920); Theophila Mikhailovna Bylina, Russian (born 1918); and Vera Petrovna Popova, Russian, as well as a manuscript written by Ivan Ionovich Ouvarov, a teacher exiled in Alexandrovskoie and an eyewitness to the events on Nazino, were published in the Tomsk newspaper *Narodnaia Tribuna* on April 17, 1993.

4. This publication was undertaken under the aegis of the Tomsk branch of the Memorial Association of the Novosibirsk Historical Institute and directed by Professor Sergei Krasilnikov. See the documents collected in *Nazinskaia Tragedia: Dokumentalnoie naucnoie izdanie* [The Nazino Tragedy: A Documented Scholarly Edition] (Tomsk: Memorial Association and Institute of History of the Siberian Branch of the Russian Academy of Science, 2002).

5. The Siberian branch of the Gulag.

6. *Nazinskaia Tragedia*, doc. 33, p. 152.

7. The OGPU (Head political office of the unified state) was the regime's political police. In reality, Genrikh Iagoda was formally only the number two man at the OGPU. Since the death in July 1926 of Feliks Dzerjinski, the founder of the Bolshevik regime's political police—which until 1922

had been called the Vecheka (or Cheka)—the OGPU had been led by Rudolf Menjinski. However, Menjinski had been suffering from a serious illness for several years, and starting in the early 1930s he gradually delegated his functions to his chief assistant, Genrikh Iagoda.

CHAPTER 1: A "GRANDIOSE PLAN"

1. The Gulag (the head management office for the camps) was created in 1930 and was directly responsible to the OGPU. It managed both the labor camps and the special villages (or "special populations") in which all the "anti-Soviet elements of the cities and countryside" were put under house arrest, by simple executive order, generally along with their families.

2. In their conception of a peasant society divided into antagonistic classes, the Bolsheviks distinguished four categories of peasants: batraks (farm workers), bedniaks (poor peasants), seredniaks (middle peasants), and kulaks (rich peasants). The criteria defining a kulak were the subject of numerous discussions within the Bolshevik party itself: the employment of a farm worker during part of the year, the possession of a piece of agricultural machinery a little more advanced than a simple plow, or two horses and/or three or four cows sufficed to classify a farmer in the infamous category of kulaks. In reality, as was to be shown by the "dekulakization" campaign pursued starting in January 1930 in connection with the collectivization of the countryside, the label "kulak" was systematically applied to any peasant who manifested hostility to collectivization. In addition, Russian Orthodox priests (called "popes"), former Czarist officials residing in the countryside, and former landlords who had remained in the USSR after the revolution were also labeled "kulaks."

3. In 1930–32, about two million kulaks had been deported. According to an OGPU report dated March 1932,

there still remained at that date in the USSR more than two hundred thousand "kulak farms" (with about a million persons). Nonetheless, as this document acknowledged, the immense majority of "kulak farms" listed (on the basis of fiscal documents dating from several years earlier) had been deserted, the farmers having fled, and thus, as contemporary political terminology put it, having "auto-dekulakized" themselves. These "escaped kulaks," the authorities claimed, had infiltrated construction sites and industrial companies in the cities. "Smoking them out" and "unmasking" them was the first order of business. See Nicolas Werth, "Le pouvoir soviétique et la paysannerie dans les rapports de la police politique, 1930–1934), *Bulletin de l'Institut d'histoire du temps présent,* no. 81–82 (2003), especially pp. 19–20, 198.

4. On "passportization," see chap. 2.

5. APRF (The Presidential Archives of the Russian Federation), collection 3, inventory 30, file 196, fols. 127–38. This manuscript text bears interesting annotations in the hand of Vyacheslav Molotov, the president of the Council of People's Commissars and the number two man in the Soviet regime ("Grossly exaggerated expenses. The deportees themselves have to be made to pay part of the costs") and Stalin ("A good plan, but we have to coordinate this plan with the decongestion of the prisons"; "all these elements should be deported for ten years"; "What has been foreseen to strengthen surveillance and prevent escapes?").

6. Clandestine depots.

7. The term used for peasants who had not yet joined kolkhozes. In early 1933, "individual peasants" represented, depending on the region, between 5 and 15 percent of the peasantry.

8. GARF (State Archives of the Russian Federation), 1235/2/1521/75–79.

9. "We are looking for the class enemy such as he is usually represented—sinister-looking people with large teeth, a fat neck, carrying an icon in their arms. We are looking

for the kulak as he is shown on posters. But there haven't been any such kulaks for a long time! The kulaks and kulakizers of today, the anti-Soviet elements in the countryside, are for the most part 'peaceful,' unctuous individuals, almost 'saints.' There's no point in looking far away from the kolkhozes—they're inside them" (J. Stalin, *Sochinenia* [Moscow: Gosudarstvennoie Izdanie Politiceskoi Literatury, 1952], vol. 13, p. 229).

10. Note from V. Balitski to G. Iagoda, January 22, 1933, APRF, 3/30/189/3–10.

11. RGASPI (Russian State Archives in Political and Social History), 558/11/45/109.

12. OGPU circular no. 50031, January 22, 1933, TsA FSB (FSB Central Archives), 2/11/6/51.

13. To avoid producing "false departure authorizations," the regional authorities prohibited, on January 25, 1933, the rural soviets and the leaders of the kolkhozes from providing peasants with the usual certificates authorizing kolkhozians to go to the city (RGASPI, 17/42/72/109–11).

14. G. Iagoda's report to Stalin, March 25, 1933, "On Steps Taken to Put an End to the Massive Exodus of Peasants," TsA FSB 2/11/6/393–94.

15. The OGPU Secret-Political Department's "special reports" for the end of 1932 and the first half of 1933 bear witness to the scope of the repression. For a selection of these documents, see Werth, "Le pouvoir soviétique et la paysannerie," pp. 214–64.

16. Supporters of Symon Petlyura (1879–1926), one of the principal leaders of the anti-Bolshevist Ukrainian nationalist movement during the civil war (1918–21). Having emigrated to Paris, Petlyura was assassinated there in May 1926 by agents of the OGPU.

17. G. Iagoda's report to Stalin, "On Cleansing Operations in the Western Border Zones of the USSR," March 26, 1933, APRF, 3/58/201/75–87.

18. Ibid.

19. That is, since the beginning of 1930, at the time that

the campaigns of forced collectivization and dekulakization were launched.

20. On March 11, 1933, the Council of People's Commissars adopted a decree on the "decongestion of places of detention" (GARF, 5446/468/141–47). See also RGASPI, 17/162/14/89–92.

21. Politburo resolution concerning the decongestion of places of detention, March 8, 1933, RGASPI, 17/162/14/76–92.

21. In 1930–32, about nine million peasants fled forced collectivization and dekulakization and settled in the cities. The Moscow and Leningrad regions alone received more than 3.5 million immigrants from the countryside.

23. This tells us a great deal about the government's supervision of the population, at least up until the beginning of the 1930s.

24. Protocol of the Politburo meeting on November 15, 1932, *Istocnik,* no. 6 (1997), p. 104.

25. On this point, cf. the Politburo resolution dated April 4, 1933: "Deport, before the season begins, by April 15 at the latest, 3,000 parasite and déclassé families in the Sochi and Tuapse districts, along with 2,000 parasite and déclassé families in the Mineralnye Vody district that are polluting these resort and holiday zones" (RGASPI, 17/162/14/108–9).

26. GARF, 9401/12/138/18.

27. The text of the secret resolution dated March 24, 1924 has been published in A. I. Kokurin and N. V. Petrov, *Lubianka, 1917–1960: Spravocnik* [The Lubianka, 1917–1960: A Guide] (Moscow: IZ. Mejdounarodnyi Fond Demokratia, 1997), pp. 179–81.

28. One of Feliks Dzerjinski's main assistants.

29. RGASPI, 76/3/390/3–4.

30. Sergei Krasilnikov, *Marginaly v postrevoliutsionnom rossiiskom obschestve* [Marginals in Postrevolutionary Russian Society] (Novosibirsk: Novosibirskii Gosudarstvennyi Universitet, 1998), p. 23.

31. Ibid., p. 49.

32. GARF, 393/2/507/52.

33. On the passportization operations, see Nathalie Moine, "Passeportisation, statistique des migrations et contrôle de l'identité sociale," *Cahiers du monde russe* 38, no. 4 (October–December 1997), pp. 587–600; Gijs Kessler, "The Passport System and State Control over Population Flows in the Soviet Union, 1932–1940," *Cahiers du monde russe* 42, no. 2–4 (April–December 2001), pp. 477–504.

34. This category had existed since 1918. Written into the first Soviet constitution, the privation of civil rights affected former high officials, both civilian and military, of the Czarist regime; members of the clergy; and all those whose revenues were judged incompatible with the principles and functioning of the new Soviet society: not only "persons living on revenues not proceeding from labor, persons drawing their income from private commerce or from an intermediary function, persons who have employed salaried workers for the purpose of making a profit," but also "persons under supervision and the mentally ill" and "persons who have been judged guilty of certain crimes." These categories were extendable and generally included the whole family of the person who had been deprived of his civil rights. In the late 1920s, there were about 3,700,000 *lichentsy* in the USSR. See N. Werth, "De quelques catégories d'exclusion dans l'URSS des années 1920 et 1930: gens du passé et éléments socialement nuisibles," in *Actes du colloque Apogée des systèmes totalitaires en Europe*, ed. S. Courtois (Paris: Éditions du Rocher, 2003), pp. 51–75.

35. Secret directive dated January 14, 1933 (GARF, 5446/15a/1096/67–75).

36. On this question, see the numerous reports in GARF, 3316/64/1227/101–2.

37. In Moscow, this represented 3.5 percent of the estimated population, and in Leningrad about 4 percent.

38. APRF, 3/58/158/116–120, cited in *Istocnik*, no. 6 (1997), p. 108.

39. Ibid.

CHAPTER 2: WESTERN SIBERIA, A LAND OF DEPORTATION

1. GARF, 9479/1s/18/1–3.

2. V. P. Danilov and S. Krasilnikov, eds., *Spetzpereselentsy v Zapadnoi Sibiri: Sbornik dokumentov* [The Special Settlers in Western Siberia: A Collection of Documents], vol. 3, *1933–1938* (Novosibirsk: Ekor, 1994), pp. 76–77.

3. V. P. Danilov and S. Krasilnikov, eds., *Spetzpereselentsy v Zapadnoi Sibiri: Sbornik dokumentov* [The Special Settlers in Western Siberia: A Collection of Documents], vol. 1 (Novosibirsk: Ekor, 1992), p. 45.

4. APRF (Presidential Archives of the Russian Federation), 3/30/196/117; Danilov and Krasilnikov, *Spetzpereselentsy v Zapadnoi Sibiri*, p. 78.

5. At the beginning of 1932, the special settlers were distributed, more or less, as follows: Urals, 485,000; Western Siberia, 300,000; Kazakhstan, 140,000; the northern region around Arkhangelsk, 120,000; Eastern Siberia, 92,000, out of a total of 1,317,000 recorded "special settlers." Knowing that during 1930 and 1931 1,803,000 peasants had been deported, the losses (deaths and escapes) were on the order of half a million, or 28 percent of the total. See V. Zemskov, *Spetzposelentsy* [The Special Settlers] (Moscow: Nauka, 2004), pp. 22–23.

6. I have consulted the French translation of Nikita Khrushchev's secret report as it is presented in Branko Lazich, *Le Rapport secret et son histoire* (Paris: Le Seuil, 1976), p. 67.

7. Under the Bolshevik regime, this term referred to those who had "enriched themselves" under the NEP thanks to the existence of a private economic sector—wholesalers, entrepreneurs, industrialists, intermediaries of all kinds.

8. On Robert Eikhe's political career, see V. Pavlova, "Robert Eikhe," *Voprosy Istorii*, no. 3 (2000), pp. 45–60.

9. M. P. Malyseva and V. S. Poznanskii, *Kazaki-bezentsy ot goloda v Zapadnoi Sibiri* [The Kazakhs Fleeing Famine in Western Siberia] (Almaty: Gylym, 1999), pp. 57–58.

10. Ibid., pp. 65–67.

11. Ibid., pp. 180–82.

12. Ibid., pp. 203–4.

13. Sixty-nine hundred kolkhozes, 40 percent of the farmers and livestock raisers, were collectivized in March, 1930; 65 percent in July 1931; and more than 90 percent by the summer of 1932, according to official documents. See N. Werth, "La famine kazakhe de 1931–1932," *Communisme*, no. 74–75 (2003), pp. 8–42.

14. On this subject, see the letter sent to Stalin by T. Ryskulov, vice-president of the Council of People's Commissars for the Russian Soviet Federated Republic on October 6, 1932 (RGASPI, 82/2/670/11–14).

15. RGASPI, 558/11/40/87.

16. Malyseva and Poznanskii, *Kazaki-bezentsy*, pp. 321–24.

17. Ibid., p. 280.

18. GARF, 5446/13a/1320/2–3.

19. David Shearer, "Social Disorder, Mass Repression, and the NKVD during the 1930s," *Cahiers du monde russe* 42, no. 2–4 (April–December 2001), p. 510.

20. Ibid., p. 511.

21. A.G. Tepliakov, "Personal i povsednevnost' Novosibirskogo UNKVD v 1936–1946" [The Personnel and Everyday Life of the NKVD's Regional Organization in Novosibirsk], *Minuvshee*, no. 21 (1997), pp. 240–44.

22. See Eric Hobsbawm, *Primitive Rebels: Studies in Archaic Forms of Social Movements in the 19th and 20th Centuries* (New York: Norton, 1965); Hobsbawm, *Bandits* (New York: New Press, 2000).

23. See Nicolas Werth, "Les rebelles primitifs en URSS," *Communisme*, no. 70–71 (2002), p. 60–91.

24. Quoted in Lynne Viola, *Peasant Rebels under Stalin: Collectivization and the Culture of Peasant Resistance* (Oxford: Oxford University Press, 1996), p. 178.

25. Nikolai Guschin and Vladimir Ilinykh, *Klassovaia bor'ba v Sibirskoi derevne, 1920-ye-seredina 1930kh gg* [Class Struggles in the Siberian Countryside from the 1920s to the First Half of the 1930s] (Novosibirsk: Novosibirskii Gosudarstvennyi Universitet, 1987), pp. 197–98.

26. Viola, *Peasant Rebels under Stalin*, p. 178.

27. V. M. Samosoudov, *Mouromtsevskoie vosstanie 1930 goda* [The Muromtsvevsk Insurrection, 1930], *Omskaia Starina* 3 (1995), pp. 141–45.

28. TsA FSB, 2/11/455/25–26.

29. On the level of the country as a whole, in 1931 17 percent of the kolkhozes were attacked by an armed group or were the victims of a "terrorist act." Cf. Sheila Fitzpatrick, *Stalin's Peasants* (Oxford: Oxford University Press, 1994), p. 234.

30. TsA FSB, 2/9/552/570–81.

31. A *poud* is a measure of weight equivalent to 16.38 kilograms.

32. V. P. Danilov and S. Krasilnikov, eds., *Spetzpereselentsy v Zapadnoi Sibiri: Sbornik dokumentov* [The Special Settlers in Western Siberia: A Collection of Documents], vol. 2, *1931–1933* (Novosibirsk: Ekor, 1993), pp. 155–56.

33. On these two great waves of dekulakization, see Werth, "Le pouvoir soviétique et la paysannerie," pp. 7–22.

34. Sergei Krasilnikov, *Serp i Molokh: Krestianskaia ssylka v Zapadnoi Sibiri v 1930-ye gody* [The Sickle and the Moloch: Peasant Deportations in Western Siberia in the 1930s] (Moscow: Rosspen, 2003), p. 76.

35. Ibid., p. 77.

36. Danilov and Krasilnikov, *Spetzpereselentsy v Zapadnoi Sibiri*, vol. 1, pp. 56–67.

37. OGPU directive, February 4, 1930.

38. Krasilnikov, *Serp y Molokh*, p. 137.

39. Ibid., p. 155.
40. Ibid., p. 156.
41. Ibid., p. 76.
42. Ibid., p. 155.
43. Danilov and Krasilnikov, *Spetzpereselentsy v Zapadnoi Sibiri,* vol. 1, p. 126.
44. V. P. Danilov et al., eds., *Tragedia Sovetskoi derevni: Kolektivisatsia i raskulacivanie: Dokumenty i materialy* [The Tragedy of the Soviet Countryside: Collectivization and Dekulakization: A Collection of Documents], vol. 3 (Moscow: Rosspen, 2000), pp. 523–25.
45. On the establishment of the Andreiev Commision and the passage from "deportation-abandonment" to "deportation-management," see Nicolas Werth, "Déplacés spéciaux et colons de travail dans la société soviétique," *Vingtième siècle: Revue d'histoire,* no. 54 (April–June 1997), pp. 340–50.
46. Danilov et al., *Tragedia Sovetskoi derevni,* vol. 2, p. 90.
47. TsA FSB, 2/10/379a/175–77.
48. Protocol of the First Meeting of the Andreiev Commission, March 18, 1931, *Istoricedskii Arxiv* [Historical Archives], no. 4 (1994), p. 153.
49. Krasilnikov, *Serpi Molokh,* pp. 87–88.
50. RGASPI, 17/120/26/241.
51. RGASPI, 17/120/26/235.
52. Danilov and Krasilnikov, *Spetzpereselentsy v Zapadnoi Sibiri,* vol. 2, p. 237.
53. GARF, 9479/1/43/6.
54. Ibid., p. 226.
55. Ibid., pp. 231–33.
56. Krasilnikov, *Serp i Molokh,* p. 161.
57. Ibid., p. 162.
58. Danilov and Krasilnikov, *Spetzpereselentsy v Zapadnoi Sibiri,* vol. 2, p. 81.
59. GARF, 9479/1/89/206–7.
60. TsA FSB, 2/11/234/5.
61. Krasilnikov, *Serp i Molokh,* p. 161.

CHAPTER 3: NEGOTIATIONS AND PREPARATIONS

1. *Nazinskaia Tragedia*, doc. 33, pp. 165–66.

2. Up to that point, special settlers had been in theory exiled and under house arrest for a period of five years, at the end of which they could recover their civil rights. Whether at the end of that period they could also return home was not specified. In 1935, when the question of the deportees' return began to arise, a secret OGPU directive specified that even after they had recovered their civil rights special settlers would not normally be allowed to return home or recuperate the goods that had been confiscated from them.

3. APRF, 3/30/196/127.

4. APRF, 3/30/196/123–24.

5. APRF, 3/30/196/126.

6. APRF, 3/30/196/127.

7. GARF, 5446/57/24/2–12.

8. TsA FSB, 2/11/1309/8–9.

9. Memo from I. Grach to G. Molchanov, March 26, 1933 (TsA FSB, 2/11/1313/84).

10. Stenographic record of the Commission of Inquiry's meeting regarding the events on the island of Nazino, in *Nazinskaia Tragedia*, doc. 33, p. 152.

11. Ibid., doc. 33, p. 103.

12. Ibid., doc. 1, p. 21.

13. Ibid.

14. Krasilnikov, *Serp i Molokh*, p. 171.

15. *Nazinskaia Tragedia*, doc. 33, p. 102.

16. For a few examples of the regulatory documents applicable to "special settlers," see GARF, 393/43a/1796/9–18; Danilov and Krasilnikov, *Spetzpereselentsy v Zapadnoi Sibiri*, vol. 1, pp. 197–205.

17. See Werth, "Déplacés spéciaux," p. 44.

18. Danilov and Krasilnikov, *Spetzpereselentsy v Zapadnoi Sibiri*, vol. 1, pp. 202–3.

19. This decree (July 3, 1931) provided that at the end

of five years, the special settlers would recover their civil rights, on the condition that they had "demonstrated by their deeds that they have ceased to combat the kolkhozes and the industrious kolkhozian peasantry, in opposition to the policy of the Soviet government," and that they "had effectively demonstrated that they were honest and conscientious workers, laboring for the country's development."

20. Danilov and Krasilnikov, *Spetzpereselentsy v Zapadnoi Sibiri*, vol. 2, p. 155.

21. *Nazinskaia Tragedia*, doc. 2, p. 23–26.

22. The komandatura was located about 150 kilometers south of Alexandrovskoie.

23. *Iz istorii zemli Tomskoi, 1930–1933: Sbornik dokumentov* [History of the Tomsk Region, 1930–1933: Document Collection] (Tomsk: Memorial, 2001), p. 352.

24. *Nazinskaia Tragedia*, doc. 1, p. 22.

25. Note that Tsepkov was not implicated in inspector Shpek's letter. He may in fact have been absent at the time of the events Shpek reported; he seems to have been summoned to Kolpachevo in September 1931 to escort a group of special settlers.

26. Krasilnikov *Serp i Molokh*, p. 173.

27. The equivalent of the senior year in high school

28. Ivan Ionych Ouvarov's account, written in 1988, was deposited in the State Archives of Tomsk Province (GATO), 1993/1/59/2–9; *Nazinskaia tragedia*, pp. 191–202.

29. Krasilnikov, *Serp i Molokh*, p. 173.

30. *Nazinskaia tragedia*, doc. 33, p. 102.

31. Ibid., p. 103.

32. A state fishing company.

33. A state crafts company.

34. Ibid., p. 105.

35. This refers to the series of meetings that were supposed to prepare for the reception of an unprecedented number of deportees. See the depositions given by Makedonskii, Gorchkov, Dolguikh, and Tsepkov before the commission of inquiry.

36. The Rybtrest combined the state fisheries, the Koust-prom the artisanal cooperatives; the Zapsiblestrest was the main forestry complex for Western Siberia, and thus the main employer of deported manpower. The Rechtrans, a state riverboating company, included all the transport boats in the Ob basin.

37. Ibid., p. 139.
38. Ibid., p. 104.
39. Ibid., p. 166.
40. Ibid., p. 105.
41. Ibid., p. 106.

CHAPTER 4: IN THE TOMSK TRANSIT CAMP

1. *Nazinskaia Tragedia*, doc. 33, p. 122.
2. TsA FSB, 2/11/763/22, 26, 28.
3. TsA FSB, 2/11/763/33.
4. TsA FSB, 2/11/763/34.
5. *Nazinskaia Tragedia*, doc. 33, p. 171.
6. A literal translation of the Russian *polutrupy*.
7. The expression used in Russian is particularly vivid, *samotekom*, in a "spontaneous flood."
8. Ibid., doc 11, pp. 36–37.
9. TsA FSB, 2/11/763/37.
10. TsA FSB, 2/11/537/255.
11. TsA FSB, 2/11/1313/201.
12. GARF, 9479/1/19/5–6.
13. TsA FSB, 2/11/537/250–59.
14. Head of the OGPU's Plenipotentiary Representation. In Western Siberia, Alexeiev held this office.
15. *Nazinskaia Tragedia*, doc. 33, p. 171.
16. TsA FSB, 2/11/1313/103.
17. RGASPI, 17/162/14/108–9.
18. TsA FSB, 2/11/1313/95.
19. TsA FSB, 2/11/766/94–109.
20. TsA FSB, 2/11/766/94–95.

21. TsA FSB, 2/11/766/96.

22. On these categories, see Nicolas Werth, "De deux catégories d'exclusion dans l'URSS des années 1920 et 1930: gens du passé et éléments socialement nuisibles," in *Actes du colloque: L'Apogée des systèmes totalitaires*, ed. S. Courtois (Paris: Ed. du Rocher, 2003), pp. 51–75.

23. TsA FSB, 2/11/537/293–96.

24. In Russian, 928 *semei i odinocek*. Naturally, formulated in this way, it is impossible to determine, even approximately, the number of persons involved. In any event, a significant proportion of the deportees were involved, a fact that was to be confirmed in the final report produced a few weeks later.

25. In bureaucratic jargon, these prohibitions on residence were called "minus 12."

26. TsA FSB, 2/11/537/292.

27. *Nazinskaia Tragedia*, doc. 33, p. 140.

28. Ibid., p. 145.

29. Cf. chap. 3.

30. Ibid., doc. 7, p. 32.

31. Ibid., doc. 33, p. 173.

32. The OGPU's labor communes, of which there were very few, represented at the beginning of the 1930s a sort of "leftover" from the Bolshevik utopia of "transforming criminals through labor" that was discussed in the early 1920s. These labor communes were reserved especially for young delinquents, abandoned children, and vagabonds.

33. TsA FSB, 2/11/763/45.

34. TsA FSB, 2/11/763/55.

35. TsA FSB, 2/11/763/84.

36. *Nazinskaia Tragedia*, doc. 33, p. 128.

37. APRF, 3/30/196/184.

38. TsA FSB, 2/11/537/240.

39. TsA FSB, 2/11/1313/101.

40. *Nazinskaia Tragedia*, doc. 33, p. 128.

41. Ibid., doc. 30, p. 90.

42. Ibid., doc 29, p. 88.

43. GARF, 9401/12/135/133.

44. Cf. chap. 1.

45. The examples cited are drawn from Velichko's letter to Stalin (published in Danilov and Krasilnikov, *Spetzpereselentsy v Zapadnoi Sibiri*, vol. 3, pp. 89–100) and the final report of the commission of inquiry headed by Kovalev (published in the same volume, pp. 100–16. Several of the Kovalev Commission's interim reports are archived in TsA FSB, 2/11/763/180–208.

46. Danilov and Krasilnikov, *Spetzpereselentsy v Zapadnoi Sibiri*, vol. 3, pp. 89–100.

47. Velichko's letter, in Danilov and Krasilnikov, *Spetzpereselentsy v Zapadnoi Sibiri*, vol. 3, p. 99.

48. Kovalev Commission Report, in ibid., p. 113.

49. "*Nabrat' i otschitatsja*," Kovalev Commission Report, October 8, 1933, TsA FSB, 2/11/763/180.

50. Velichko's letter, in Danilov and Krasilnikov, *Spetzpereselentsy v Zapadnoi Sibiri*, vol. 3, p. 96.

51. This famous decree, personally instigated by Stalin, established a penalty of ten years in a camp (and in certain circumstances, the death penalty) for theft or waste of "social property." Rapidly nicknamed "the five ears of grain law" (most of the people sentenced under it were starving kolkhozians who had stolen a few ears of grain in the collective fields), this law, which affected more than 100,000 persons as soon as it began to be applied, immediately aroused great social resentment against the regime.

52. TsA FSB, 2/11/763/80.

53. Kovalev Commission Report, in Danilov and Krasilnikov, *Spetzpereselentsy v Zapadnoi Sibiri*, vol. 3, pp. 112–13.

54. *Nazinskaia Tragedia*, doc. 33, p. 123.

55. Ibid., p. 176.

CHAPTER 5. NAZINO

1. *Nazinskaia Tragedia*, doc. 33, p. 107.

2. Ibid., p. 117.

3. Ibid., p. 118.

4. Ibid., doc. 32, p. 101.

5. Ibid., doc. 32, p. 116.

6. Ibid., p.108.

7. Ibid., p. 101. On this point, the record of the meeting of the District Committee of the Party (May 5, 1933) confirms Vlassov's deposition.

8. *Nazinskaia Tragedia*, doc. 8, p. 33–34.

9. Ibid., doc. 33, p. 124.

10. Ibid., p. 125.

11. Velichko's letter, in Danilov and Krasilnikov, *Spetzpereselentsy v Zapadnoi Sibiri*, vol. 3, p. 90.

12. *Nazinskaia Tragedia*, doc. 33, p. 125.

13. This expression refers to the title of the famous Article 2 of March 2, 1930, in which Stalin criticized local officials for having yielded to the "dizziness of success" and having committed numerous abuses and "distortions of the principle of voluntary service" in the course of collectivization.

14. Ibid., p. 128.

15. Ibid., p. 112.

16. Ibid., p. 126.

17. Velichko's testimony; the report submitted by Kiselev, the accountant for the Alexandro-Vakhovskaia komandatura, who was present on the site, to the head of the Siblag's accounting department, May 19, 1933 (*Nazinskaia Tragedia*, doc. 10, pp. 35–36); the report (undated) by Kobulaiev, head of the convoy, to Kuznetsov, head of the Tomsk transit camp (*Nazinskaia Tragedia*, doc. 15, pp. 43–45); Tsepkov's depositions before the Commission of Inquiry (*Nazinskaia Tragedia*, doc. 33, pp. 110–14).

18. *Nazinskaia Tragedia*, doc. 33, pp. 110–11.

19. Ibid.

20. Velichko's letter, in Danilov and Krasilnikov, *Spetzpereselentsy v Zapadnoi Sibiri*, vol. 3, p. 91; Kolubaiev's testimony, in *Nazinskaia Tragedia*, doc. 15, p. 44.

21. Velichko's testimony, ibid.; Kolubaiev's testimony, ibid.

22. *Nazinskaia Tragedia*, doc. 33, p. 111.

23. Ibid., doc. 15, p. 44.

24. Ibid., doc. 33, p. 118.

25. Velichko's letter, in Danilov and Krasilnikov, *Spetzpereselentsy v Zapadnoi Sibiri*, vol. 3, p. 92.

26. *Nazinskaia Tragedia*, Ouvarov's account, p. 198.

27. Danilov and Krasilnikov, *Spetzpereselentsy v Zapadnoi Sibiri*, vol. 3, pp. 80–81.

28. Contrary to Taissa M. Chokareva's testimony, which mentions the trafficking in gold crowns taken from cadavers, there was no Torgsin in Alexandrovskoie. The traffickers sold their "production" to the Torgsin in Tomsk. The network of Torgsin stores was under the control of the People's Commisariat for Internal Affairs.

29. "One deportee had tried to get two rations of flour. "'Stand over there,' said the guard Khodov, and then shot him in the head with his revolver (he executed many people in this way before being relieved of his office at his own request)" (Velichko, in Danilov and Krasilnikov, *Spetzpereselentsy v Zapadnoi Sibiri*, vol. 3, p. 92).

30. Kovalev Commission's report, TsA FSB, 2/11/763/185–86; Danilov and Krasilnikov, *Spetzpereselentsy v Zapadnoi Sibiri*, vol. 3, p. 114.

31. Velichko's letter, in Danilov and Krasilnikov, *Spetzpereselentsy v Zapadnoi Sibiri*, vol. 3, p. 94.

32. The expression is Moshe Lewin's. See "L'arrière-plan social du stalinisme," in Moshe Lewin, *La Formation du système soviétique* (Paris: Gallimard, 1987), p. 381.

33. *Nazinskaia Tragedia*, doc. 33, p. 161.

34. Nina Lugovskaia, *Journal d'une écolière soviétique* (Paris: Robert Laffont, 2005), p. 77.

35. Cf. for example the "Rapport-compilation d'extraits de lettres envoyées aux recrues de l'armée Rouge" [Report-compilation of extracts from letters sent to recruits in the

Red Army], dated March 1, 1933, in Werth, "Le pouvoir soviétique et la paysannerie," pp. 234–40.

36. Cf. chap. 2.

37. Marc Bloch, "Réflexions d'un historien sur les fausses nouvelles de la guerre," in *Mélanges historiques*, vol. 1 (Paris, EHESS, 1983), p. 54. For an analysis of the phenomenon of rumors applied to Stalin's USSR, I refer the reader to my article "Rumeurs défaitistes et apocalyptiques dans l'URSS des années 1920 et 1930," *Vingtième siècle: Revue d'histoire*, no. 71 (July–September 2001), pp. 25–37.

38. See, for example, the instructions issued by the head of the GPU of Ukraine, Vsevolod Balitski, dated March 22, 1933, ordering his subordinates to inform the Party's regional officials of "questions regarding food-supply difficulties" only in oral form, "in order to prevent handwritten notes from circulating among apparatuses and thus giving rise to various rumors regarding an alleged famine or acts of anthropophagy." See Werth, "Le pouvoir soviétique et la paysannerie," introduction, p. 35.

39. See Kolubaiev's report on his visit to the island of Nazino on May 20, *Nazinskaia Tragedia*, doc. 15, p. 44.

40. V. P. Danilov, S. Krasilnikov (eds.), vol. 3, pp. 80–81. According to another account, the day before 137 bodies had been collected by deportees working as gravediggers in exchange for bread rations (*Nazinskaia Tragedia*, doc. 33, p. 158).

41. Ibid.

42. Ibid., doc. 19, pp. 52–53.

43. Ibid., doc. 33, p. 159.

44. Ibid., doc. 16, p. 46.

45. Ibid., doc 33, p. 160.

46. A contraction of the terms "atavism" and "onanism"!

47. Ibid., doc 30, p. 97.

48. Jacques Rossi, *Le Manuel du Goulag* (Paris: Le Cherche Midi, 1997), p. 283.

49. Testimonies given by Maria Nikitichna Akhtina, Nazino, July 21, 1989; Taissia Mikhailovna Chokareva, July 21,

1989; Theophila Mikhailovna Bylina, July 21, 1989; and Natalia Dimitrievna Tanasakova, July 22, 1989, all published in *Narodnaia Tribuna* (Tomsk), April 17, 1993.

50. Bylina testimony.

51. Bylina and Tanasakova testimonies.

52. TsA FSB, 2/11/763/257–58; *Nazinskaia Tragedia*, doc. 30, p. 97.

53. Significantly, the question of cannibalism is dealt with in the part of Dolguikh's report entitled "Political Situation."

54. *Nazinskaia Tragedia*, doc. 30, pp. 96–97.

55. Ibid.

56. Ibid., doc. 26, pp. 79–80; Ivan Ouvarov's account, in ibid., pp. 197–99.

57. Krasilnikov, *Serp i Moloch*, p. 104.

58. *Nazinskaia Tragedia*, doc. 26, p. 80.

59. Ivan Ouvarov's account, in ibid., p. 199.

60. Report submitted by the medical staff of the Alexandro-Vakhovskaia komandatura regarding the situation on the island of Nazino, June 6, 1933, in *Nazinskaia Tragedia*, doc. 17, p. 50.

61. Resolution of the Office of the District Committee of the Party of Alexandrovskoie regarding Comrade Tsepkov's report, "On the Reception and Settlement of Déclassé Elements," May 29, 1933, in *Nazinskaia Tragedia*, doc. 14, pp. 41–43.

62. *Nazinskaia Tragedia*, doc. 16, pp. 45–49.

63. Ibid., doc. 16, pp. 47–48; doc. 33, pp. 114–15.

64. Ibid., doc 20, p. 54.

65. In his letter to Stalin, Velichko cites the case of a boat that left the island of Nazino with 78 deportees aboard and arrived four days later with 12 survivors (in Danilov and Krasilnikov, *Spetzpereselentsy v Zapadnoi Sibiri*, vol. 3, p. 93).

66. Concerning the number of dead counted on the island, the figures vary from 1,473 (report submitted by Reschikov, assistant head of the Executive Committee of the soviets of Western Siberia, between June 12 and June 16,

in *Nazinskaia Tragedia,* doc. 20, p. 54) to 1,970 (report of the Siblag Commission, June 21, 1933, in *Nazinskaia Tragedia,* doc. 22, p. 58).

67. Ivan Ouvarov's testimony, *Nazinskaia Tragedia,* p. 200.

68. The count, ordered following the visit to Nazino by the head of the Siblag's Department of Special Settlements, I. Dolguikh, mentioned 2,809 disappearances. According to the note Tsepkov sent on June 29, "the 2,809 missing individuals are considered to be fugitives, with the exception of 455 bodies found on the island of Nazino and 991 bodies found in the surrounding taiga." See *Nazinskaia Tragedia,* doc. 23, p. 61.

69. GANO, P-3/2/363/63.

70. *Nazinskaia Tragedia,* doc. 33, p. 149–50. In addition, toward the end of August Dolguikh wrote a long report on his mission, which complements his declarations before the commission of inquiry. Cf. TsA FSB, 2/11/763/250–59.

71. Dolguikh's report before the Commission of Inquiry, in *Nazinskaia Tragedia,* doc. 33, p. 149. In his written report, Dolguikh described in detail, like a zealous bureaucrat, what he had been able to collect. A real catalog of penury: "190 iron shovels, 217 meters of fabric, 50 pairs of worn shoes, 330 used lightweight overcoats, 2,000 needles, 259 spools of thread, 1,000 buttons, 200 thimbles, 98 used fur hats, 3,750 wooden spoons, 15 cases of windowpanes, 519 kilos of dry biscuits, 2,070 kilos of salt fish, 5,394 kilos of bread" (TsA FSB, 2/11/763/253).

72. *Nazinskaia Tragedia,* doc. 30, pp. 93–94.

73. Ibid., p. 90.

74. Ibid., pp. 91–92.

75. Ibid., doc. 22, pp. 57–61.

76. According to data collected by the Office of Special Settlements, in the course of 1933 nearly 120,000 deportees "disappeared" in Western Siberia (as opposed to 74,000 in 1932). The statistical tables distinguish between "deaths recorded" (26,709), "escapes recorded" (49,718),

and "other departures" (43,048). See Zemskov, *Spetzperelentsy*, pp. 23–25.

77. See chap. 4.

78. GANO, P-3/2/363/117.

79. TsA FSB, 2/11/763/143.

80. GARF, 9479/1/19/7.

81. As noted in a Siblag report dated October, 1933, "the special contingent of Gypsies from the Moscow region is no longer registered as such, almost all of its elements having escaped and disappeared." See Iu. A. Poliakov and V. B. Jiromskaia, eds., *Naselenie Rossii v XX veke* [The Population of Russia in the Twentieth Century], vol. 1, 1900–1939 (Moscow: Ed. Rosspen, 2000), p. 308.

82. GARF, 9479/1/19/9.

83. *Nazinskaia Tragedia*, doc. 24, pp. 62–66.

84. Ibid., p. 63.

85. Ibid., p. 65.

86. Ibid., p. 66.

87. Ibid.

88. TsA FSB, 2/11/763/104. Cf., on the same note, the report the head of the Siblag sent on June 28, 1933, to G. Iagoda and M. Berman, TsA FSB 2/11/763/106.

89. Letter from the journalist-propagandist V. Velichko to K. I. Levits, R. Eikhe, and J. V. Stalin, in Danilov and Krasilnikov, *Spetzperelentsy v Zapadnoi Sibiri*, vol. 3, pp. 89–100.

90. To the 6,100 individuals unloaded on Nazino on May 18 and May 26, 1933, Velichko added "500–700 . . . additional individuals brought from other komandaturas to settlement sites along the Nazina River" (ibid., p. 95).

91. Before being admitted as a member of the Party, the candidate had to wait for a period whose length was determined by his social origin (in general, six months for workers, a year for peasants, two years for employees). In the meantime, he received a card indicating that he was a "candidate for the Communist Party."

92. *Nazinskaia Tragedia*, doc. 33, p. 138.

93. Velichko's letter, in Danilov and Krasilnikov, *Spetzperelentsy v Zapadnoi Sibiri*, vol. 3, p. 99.

94. RGASPI, 17/163/992/20.

95. Danilov and Krasilnikov, *Spetzperelentsy v Zapadnoi Sibiri*, vol. 3, p. 107.

96. Ibid., p. 108.

97. On this point, the commission largely adopted the conclusions of a long report that had been submitted to it by the secretary of the Party organization of the Narym Region, Levits. In order to remedy the "loss of class feeling" among the local Communists, Levits proposed to organize a network of small komandatura libraries provided with an abundance of "Party literature" and newspapers (see Krasilnikov, *Serp v Moloch*, pp. 179–80).

98. Danilov and Krasilnikov, *Spetzperelentsy v Zapadnoi Sibiri*, vol. 3, p. 110.

99. Including about 6,100 unloaded on the island of Nazino on May 18 and May 26, and about 4,200 sent from Tomsk in three convoys (June 29, July 14 and July 18, 1933).

100. The regional authorities of the OGPU had already tried to negotiate the transfer of nearly 2,000 deportees to the mines of the Kuzbass basin, but the leaders of the Kuzbassugol' had categorically refused this labor force, which nonetheless could be exploited mercilessly, preferring to employ "exclusively hard-working ex-kulaks" (see telegram sent by Alexeiev, head of the OGPU for Western Siberia, to G. Iagoda, September 29, 1933, TsA FSB, 2/11/763/175).

101. Danilov and Krasilnikov, *Spetzperelentsy v Zapadnoi Sibiri*, vol. 3, p. 115.

102. For example, cf. the different statistical tables of the Siblag's accounting department regarding the movements (arrivals and departures) of deportees who had passed through the transit camps in Tomsk, Omsk, and Achinsk and sent to the komandaturas of Western Siberia during the "deportation campaign" of 1933 (GANO, 3/2/363/36,

37, 117, 118, 162–65, 172–75). I thank Professor S. Krasil-nikov for having sent me these documents.

103. Danilov and Krasilnikov, *Spetzpereselentsy v Zapadnoi Sibiri*, vol. 3, p. 115.

104. TsA FSB, 2/11/763/181.

105. TsA FSB, 2/11/763/175.

106. Ibid., p. 177.

107. I have not been able to determine the nature of the sanctions imposed on them.

108. TsA FSB, 2/11/763/203–6.

CONCLUSION

1. On the processes of decivilization, cf. Stephen Mendel, "L'envers de la médaille: les processus de décivilisation," in *Elias, la politique et l'histoire*, ed. C. Lacroix and J. Guarrigou (Paris: La Découverte, 1997), pp. 213–36.

2. See, for example, OGPU directive no. 44–21, January 30, 1930: "On Operational Measures of Liquidation of the Kulaks as a Class," sent to all regional leaders by the political police. This directive assigned to each region "quotas of dekulakization in the first and second categories." Initially, 60,000 "kulaks of the first category," defined as "engaged in counterrevolutionary activities" or "particularly hardened," were to be arrested and transferred to a labor camp following a summary extrajudicial procedure. Initially, 154,000 "kulaks of the second category," just as arbitrarily defined as "exploiting peasants, but less actively engaged in counterrevolutionary activities," were to be arrested and deported, along with their families, to special villages set up in remote and inhospitable parts of the country.

3. I borrow this expression from Lynne Viola. See Lynne Viola, "The Aesthetic of Stalinist Planning and the World of Special Villages," *Kritika* 4, no. 1 (2003), pp. 101–28.

4. The "Gulag Special Settlements" collection (GARF, 9479/1) preserves thousands of pages of this bureaucratic and regulatory literature.

5. GARF, 9479/1/3/23–24.

6. Particularly enlightening regarding the frustration of political and police officials unable to control the development of the operations and the appropriate choice of the victims of dekulakization are, for example, these remarks written by Iagoda in 1930 on the reports detailing the various categories of individuals arrested: "Middle Volga and Leningrad have not understood our instructions or do not want to understand them. They have to be forced to understand. We are not cleansing the territories of priests, merchants, and others. If they write "others," that means that they don't know whom they're arresting. We have plenty of time to get rid of priests and merchants, we have to hit the precise target: kulaks and counterrevolutionary kulaks" (TsA FSB, 2/8/41/40).

7. See Moine, "Passeportisation, statistique des migrations et contrôle de l'identité sociale."

8. Max Weber, *Economy and Society*, vol. 1 (Berkeley: University of California Press, 1978), p. 54.

9. On the complex alchemy linking modernization with the resurgence of archaisms, cf. Moshe Lewin's brilliant analyses in *La Formation du système soviétique* (Paris: Gallimard, 1987), especially chaps. 11 and 12.

EPILOGUE

1. On January 1, 1933, 1,142,000 special settlers were on record. Since the beginning of the mass deportations in 1930, the losses had been colossal: about two million persons had been deported in 1930–32; thus more than 40 percent had disappeared in three years. No centralized statistics having been recorded until the beginning of 1932, it is impossible, up to that point, to tell how many died and how many escaped. See V. Zemskov, *Spetsposelentsy v SSSR, 1930–1960* [Special Settlers in the USSR, 1930–1960] (Moscow: Nauka, 2003), pp. 20–23.

2. Ibid.

3. Among the many document collections on everyday life in the special settlements during the first half of the 1930s, see in particular T. Tsarevskaia, ed., *Spetzperelentsy,* vol. 2, *Istoria Stalinskogo Gulaga* [History of Stalin's Gulag], 6 vols. (Moscow: Rosspen, 2004).

4. GARF, 9479/1/16/15. Numerous analogous reports for the main regions where special settlers were concentrated (the North, Siberia, the Urals, Kazakhstan) in GARF 9479/1/7–10. Cf. also N. Slavko, ed., *Kultatskaia ssylka na Urale, 1930–1936* [The Kulak Exile in the Urals, 1930–1936] (Moscow, 1995); V. V. Alexeiev, *Raskulechennye spetspereselentsy na Urale* [Dekulakized Peasants in the Urals] (Ekaterinburg, 1993); G. F. Dobronozhenko and L. S. Shabalova, eds., *Spetsposelki v Komi oblasti* [Special Villages in the Komi Republic] (Syktyvkar, 1997); Lynne Viola, "La famine de 1932–1933 en Union soviétique," *Vingtième siècle: Revue d'histoire,* no. 88 (October–December 2005), pp. 5–22.

5. Between January and June 1933, the supply norms for special settlers were decreased by 50 percent for flour and dried fish, 70 percent for sugar. In May and June 1933, the "regulation alimentary ration" (*paiok*) for a working adult deportee was 6 kilos of flour per month, 800 grams of dried fish, and 300 grams of sugar. Other foodstuffs, such as meat, dairy products, and vegetables, which the deportees were supposed to produce by themselves in the framework of the plan for "alimentary self-sufficiency," were completely absent from the meager assortment making up the *paiok.*

6. GARF, 9479/1/89/216. For a detailed analysis of these figures, see Iu. A. Poliakov and V. B. Jiromskaia, eds., *Naselenie Rossii v XX veke* [The Russian Population in the Twentieth Century], vol. 1 (Moscow: Rosspen, 2000), pp. 279–80.

7. The number of detainees incarcerated in prisons was to be cut in half within two months, those serving short terms being released, and those serving terms of three to five years sent to labor villages. Only those serving terms of more than five years were to be transferred to labor

220 Notes to Epilogue

camps. Text of the circular of May 8, 1933, in Danilov et al., *Tragedia sovetskoi derevni*, vol. 3, pp. 746–50.

8. GARF, 5446/57/25/161–66 (Resolution of the Council of People's Commissars, August 21, 1933).

9. In 1935–36, several tens of thousands of people belonging to ethnic minorities (Finns, Poles, Germans) were deported from the USSR's western border regions (around Leningrad and in western Ukraine) in connection with operations whose goal was to "cleanse" and "make secure" the USSR's frontiers. In September and October 1937, the whole of the Korean minority in the Vladivostok region (170,000 persons) was deported to Kazakhstan. Officially, these "administratively transferred" contingents—to use the then-current bureaucratic terminology—were not *stricto sensu* conflated with the special settlers who had been expropriated and deprived of their civil rights. See Nicolas Werth, "Les déportations de populations suspectes dans les espaces russes et soviétiques, 1914–1953: Violences de guerre, ingénierie sociale, excision ethno-historique," *Communisme*, no. 78/79 (2004), pp. 11–43.

10. Starting in 1940, the population of the special settlements began to grow rapidly once again, following the deportation of several hundred thousand Poles and Balts from the territories annexed by the USSR through the secret protocol of the German-Soviet pact signed on August 23, 1939.

11. Rising from 334,000 detainees at the beginning of 1933 to 510,000 in January 1934. On the Gulag's statistics, see Poliakov and Jiromskaia, *Naselenie Rossii v XX veke*, pp. 311–30.

12. Ibid., p. 326.

13. GARF, 1235/2/1650/27–35. For a more detailed analysis of the various sentences imposed on persons arrested in connection with passportization operations, see Werth, "De quelques catégories d'exclusion," pp. 72–73.

14. GARF, 5446/15a/1071/16–20.

15. With the reform of the People's Commissariat for Internal Affairs in July 1934, the police commissions (*troiki*)

set up at the time of the passportization campaign had been temporarily abolished. The matters they dealt with were referred to the courts, which were completely over-whelmed by the influx of files.

16. RGASPI, 558/2/155/66–67.

17. GARF, 9401/1/4157/203.

18. GARF, 8131/38/6/62–64. Cf. David Shearer, "Social Disorder, Mass Repression and the NKVD during the 1930s," *Cahiers du Monde russe* 42, nos. 2–4 (April–December 2001), p. 524.

19. See Werth, "Les rebelles primitifs en URSS."

20. On this subject, see the reports sent by the head of the NKVD in Western Siberia, S. M. Mironov, to R. Eikhe (May and June 1937) and N. Yezhov (early July 1937), published in *Trud*, August 2, 1997, p. 5.

21. Shearer, "Social Disorder, Mass Repression and the NKVD," p. 531.

22. A three-member extrajudicial commission composed of the First Secretary of the regional organization of the Communist Party, the regional head of the NKVD, and the regional prosecutor. The sentence, which was rendered be-hind closed doors, without any defense for the accused, and was not subject to appeal, was immediately carried out. In a single session, one troika handed down several hundred verdicts.

23. Danilov et al., *Tragedia sovetskoi derevni*, vol. 5, pt. 1, p. 146.

24. The quotas for the Moscow region were 35,000 (in-cluding 5,000 in the first category); for the Leningrad re-gion 14,000 (including 4,000 in the first category); for Western Siberia (the provinces of Novosibirsk, Omsk, and the Altai) 20,500 (including 14,000 in the first category); for the Urals 16,000 (including 5,500 in the first category); for the Azov-Black Sea region 13,000 (including 5,000 in the first category). The NKVD's operational order no. 00447 was published for the first time in *Trud*, June 4, 1992. For an analysis of the "Great Terror" and the role

of the "operations of mass repression" in this paroxysmal episode of Stalinist violence, I refer the reader to my article "Repenser la Grande Terreur," *Le Débat*, no. 122 (November–December 2002), pp. 118–39.

25. Ibid., p. 124.

26. This term was popularized by Robert Conquest in his pioneering work *The Great Terror: Stalin's Purge of the Thirties* (New York: Macmillan, 1968). Not having any access to Soviet archives, Conquest, using sources then available in the West, emphasized the repression directed against the Communist elites, political, military, and economic officials, and the intelligentsia at the expense of the mass repression directed against socially harmful elements. The repression of the elites, largely popularized by the regime itself (see the great "Moscow trials"), affected only a negligible proportion of the total number of victims of the Great Terror (a few tens of thousands out of a million and a half persons arrested by the NKVD, of which about 800,000 were shot).

27. *Trud*, June 4, 1992, p. 1. English translation of order no. 00447 in J. Arch Getty and O. Naumov, eds., *The Road to Terror: Stalin and the Self-destruction of the Bolsheviks, 1932–1939* (New Haven: Yale University Press, 1999), pp. 473–78.

28. GARF, 8131/37/131/36–39.

29. S. Mironov was head of the NKVD for the provinces of Novosibirsk and the Altai, G. Gorbatch was the head for the province of Omsk. Beginning in September 1937, Gorbatch became the overall head of the regional NKVD.

30. Quoted in A. A. Petrushin, *My ne znaem poscady: Sbornik dokumentov* [We Know No Pity: Document Collection] (Tiumen: Memorial, 1999), pp. 137–38.

31. Danilov et al., *Tragedia sovetskoi derevni*, vol. 5, pt. 1, doc. 214, p. 326.

32. Calculated on the basis of Danilov et al., *Tragedia Sovetskoi derevni*, vol. 5, pt. 1, doc. 264 (provinces of Novosibirsk and the Altai); V. M. Samosudov, *Bolshoi terror v Omskom Priirtychie* [The Great Terror in the Region of Omsk and Irtysh] (Omsk, 1998), pp. 120, 122.

33. This expression referred to the ordinary police, as opposed to the political police.

34. For example, cf. the way in which the NKVD of the Altai region operated in October and November 1937 in "filling the quotas" of operation no. 00447 (GARF 8131/ 32/6329/27–32).

35. As is suggested by the brief biographical notices summing up in a few lines "the itinerary of marginalization" followed by the Great Terror's victims, most of them had for years been accumulating all the attributes of social pariahs. They had been deported at the beginning of the 1930s, had often escaped from the place where they had been under house arrest, had tried to change their identities, had been put on file by the police, arrested, and during the first half of the 1930s they had often been sentenced, as "hardened violators of the passport rules," speculators, ex-kulaks, or déclassé elements to terms in a camp. See the numerous "memoirs of victims of repression" that have appeared, province by province, in Russia since the middle of the 1990s. For a bibliographical list of these sources, see Rolf Binner, Marc Junge, and Terry Martin, "The Great Terror in the Provinces of the USSR: A Cooperative Bibliography," *Cahiers du Monde russe* 42, no. 2–4 (April–December 2001), pp. 679–95.

HUMAN RIGHTS AND CRIMES AGAINST HUMANITY
Eric D. Weitz, Series Editor

This series provides a forum for publication and debate on the most pressing issues of modern times: the establishment of human rights standards and, at the same time, their persistent violation. It features a broad understanding of human rights, one that encompasses democratic citizenship as well as concerns for social, economic, and environmental justice. Its understanding of crimes against humanity is similarly broad, ranging from large-scale atrocities like ethnic cleansings, genocides, war crimes, and various forms of human trafficking to lynchings, mass rapes, and torture. Some books in the series are more historically oriented and explore particular events and their legacies. Others focus on contemporary concerns, like instances of forced population displacements or indiscriminate bombings. Still others provide serious reflection on the meaning and history of human rights or on the reconciliation efforts that follow major human rights abuses. Chronologically, the series runs from around 1500, the onset of the modern era marked by European colonialism abroad and the Atlantic slave trade, to the present. Geographically, it takes in every area of the globe. It publishes significant works of original scholarship and major interpretations by historians, human rights practitioners, legal scholars, social scientists, philosophers, and journalists. An important goal is to bring issues of human rights and their violations to the attention of a wide audience and to stimulate discussion and debate in the public sphere as well as among scholars and in the classroom. The knowledge that develops from the series will also, we hope, help promote human rights standards and prevent future crimes against humanity.

Echoes of Violence: Letters from a War Reporter by Carolin Emcke

Cannibal Island: Death in a Siberian Gulag by Nicolas Werth, translated by Steven Rendall